Copyright © 2013, 2005, 1997 PAGODA Academy, Inc.

All rights reserved. No part of this publication may be reproduced, stored in a retrieval system, or transmitted in any form or by any means, electronic, mechanical, photocopying, recording or otherwise, without the prior written permission of the copyright holder and the publisher.

Published by PAGODA Books
PAGODA Books is the professional language publishing company of the PAGODA Education Group.
19F, PAGODA Tower, 419, Gangnam-daero,
Seocho-gu, Seoul, 06614, Rep. of KOREA
www.pagodabook.com

1st Published 2013
14th Impression 2025
Printed in the Republic of Korea

ISBN 978-89-6281-504-7 (13740)

Publisher | Seo-Jin Park
Writers | Judson Wright, Lee Robinson
Editor | Hana Sakuragi
Advisor | Seo-Jin Park
Illustrator | Dae Ho Kim

Acknowledgements
Sang Hee Kang, Daniel Kim, Lionel Ouellette, Song Rim Park, and Gemma Young for their support
James Bialek, Wade Chilcoat, Patrick Farrell, Sara Green, Niki Merriman, Nathan Morris, and Meredith Watson for trialing and feedback
Eric Busch, Dayna Garwacki, Benjamin Huber, Nathan Morris, and Gemma Young for voice recording

A defective book may be exchanged at the store where you purchased it.

To Our Students

• • •

The SLE program is a conversation program for adult and young adult students who want to improve their English in an enjoyable, effective, and authentic way. It allows students to use English in a variety of contexts with an emphasis on many different useful functions. Our goal is to improve your confidence in your speaking, listening, reading and writing ability while improving your vocabulary and grammar skills. We will help you to understand not only the "How" but the "Why" of English usage.

The SLE Level 1 textbook series is meant for students with a general understanding of the basics of English conversation skills. The material in this book focuses on building students' ability to perform basic functions and use essential structures.

Contents SLE 1B

To Our Students | 3
Format of the Book | 6
Goals for the Course | 7
Meet the Jones Family | 8

UNIT 1
Don't I Know You?

Introductions & Reporting

▶ 11

LESSON 1 | 12
LESSON 2 | 18

UNIT 2
Wish You Were Here

Opinions & Suggestions

▶ 29

LESSON 1 | 30
LESSON 2 | 38

UNIT 3
The Human Environment

Comparisons & Homes

▶ 51

LESSON 1 | 52
LESSON 2 | 62

UNIT 4
Frequently Asked Questions

Preferences & Frequency

▶ 75

LESSON 1 | 76
LESSON 2 | 84

UNIT 5
Where Were You When

Moments in Time

▶ 95

LESSON 1 | 96
LESSON 2 | 102

Listening Dialogues | 206
Glossary | 210

UNIT 6
Mixed Feelings
Feelings & Friends
▶ **111**

UNIT 7
Give Me a Hint
Purpose & Reason
▶ **131**

UNIT 8
Taking It All In
The Senses
▶ **153**

UNIT 9
What Seems to Be the Problem?
Problems & Solutions
▶ **173**

UNIT 10
Looking Back
Bringing It All Together
▶ **191**

LESSON 1 | 112
LESSON 2 | 118

LESSON 1 | 132
LESSON 2 | 140

LESSON 1 | 154
LESSON 2 | 162

LESSON 1 | 174
LESSON 2 | 180

LESSON 1 | 192

Format of the Book:

Overall Format
There are ten units in this textbook, each with its own focus. In each unit there are two individual lessons. The focus of the lesson is either grammatical or topical. Each unit consists of the following elements:

Warm Up
The warm up for each lesson has its own purpose. The lesson one warm up is used as an opportunity to start thinking about the topic. The lesson two warm up is used as a quick review of the language used in the first lesson and a bridge to the second lesson.

WARM UP
PART 1
Brainstorm questions related to the foll
- Name
- School/Work
- Age
- Hobby
- Home

Listening
Each listening follows the story of the Jones family and relates to the unit topic and language points used in that unit. Each listening requires the student to make predictions based on illustrations and use communicative language to discuss what they have heard.

Listening TRACK 4-5
1. Look at the images below and guess whic on her vacation.
2. Check the box related to the activity tha nation of Kipi Kipi.

Language Point
Language points occur at the start of any activity where a specific grammar or function point is used in that activity and needs to be explained to the student.

Activities
Each lesson consists of a structured activity, a communicative activity, and a task based activity. All units include a "Bonus activity" that can add to the lesson.

Discussion Questions
Each lesson has a short series of discussion questions that relate to the topic and encourage the use of asking follow-up questions.

Boxes
Several boxes are found throughout the text and have different functions:

- **Recycle Box**
Reminds the student of language points they have used previously in SLE.
- **Third Wheel**
Gives a suggestion of how students can perform an activity with an extra student.
- **Do You Know?**
Explains the reason why language is used in a specific way.
- **Do You Remember?**
Reminds students of vocabulary from a previous lesson.
- **Tip**
Gives a tip on how the student can acquire the language easier.

Segue Activity
The segue activity consists of a reading that relates to the topic of the listening, discussion questions which check the comprehension of the reading, and a short writing task on the topic.

Goals for the Course:

1 Use the following grammatical structures:

- **a** Reported speech
- **b** Modals of suggestion
- **c** Comparatives and superlatives
- **d** *When* and *while* to discuss the past
- **e** Adjectives to describe feelings
- **f** *Would* to describe possibility
- **g** *Used for* and *used to* to describe purpose
- **h** Sense verbs

2 Perform the following functions:

- **a** Asking for additional information
- **b** Asking for and giving opinions
- **c** Talking about differences and similarities
- **d** Describing frequency
- **e** Giving reasons for preferences
- **f** Asking about what happened
- **g** Expressing necessity
- **h** Talking about the senses
- **i** Asking about problems and expressing complaints

- Making recommendations and suggestions
- Giving advice
- Comparisons

Did You Know?
"Get in" vs. "Get on"

These two phrasal verbs are very similar! When talking about travel, "get on" is generally used for vehicles in which you can stand, and "get in" is used for vehicles in which you must sit.

Need to Know:

- **to be fired**
Lucas **was fired** from his job because he stole money from the safe.

- **to be laid off**
Because of budget cuts, thirty employees **were laid off** last week.

- **to retire**
My parents **retired** when they were 60-years-old.

- **to quit**
She **quit** her job because the salary was too low.

- **to get promoted**
When Fred **got promoted**, he received a higher salary.

3rd wheel
If you are the third member in this activity, interrupt the speakers politely, offer your own greeting, and join the conversation.

Tip What's a follow-up question? Asking a follow-up question is an important part of keeping a conversation going. By asking follow-up questions you are showing interest in the conversation.

objectives:
- Use indirect questions
- Listen to a story about scams

Do You Remember?
creativity
patience
dedication
honesty
social skills
organization
judgment
passion

• see glossary for definitions

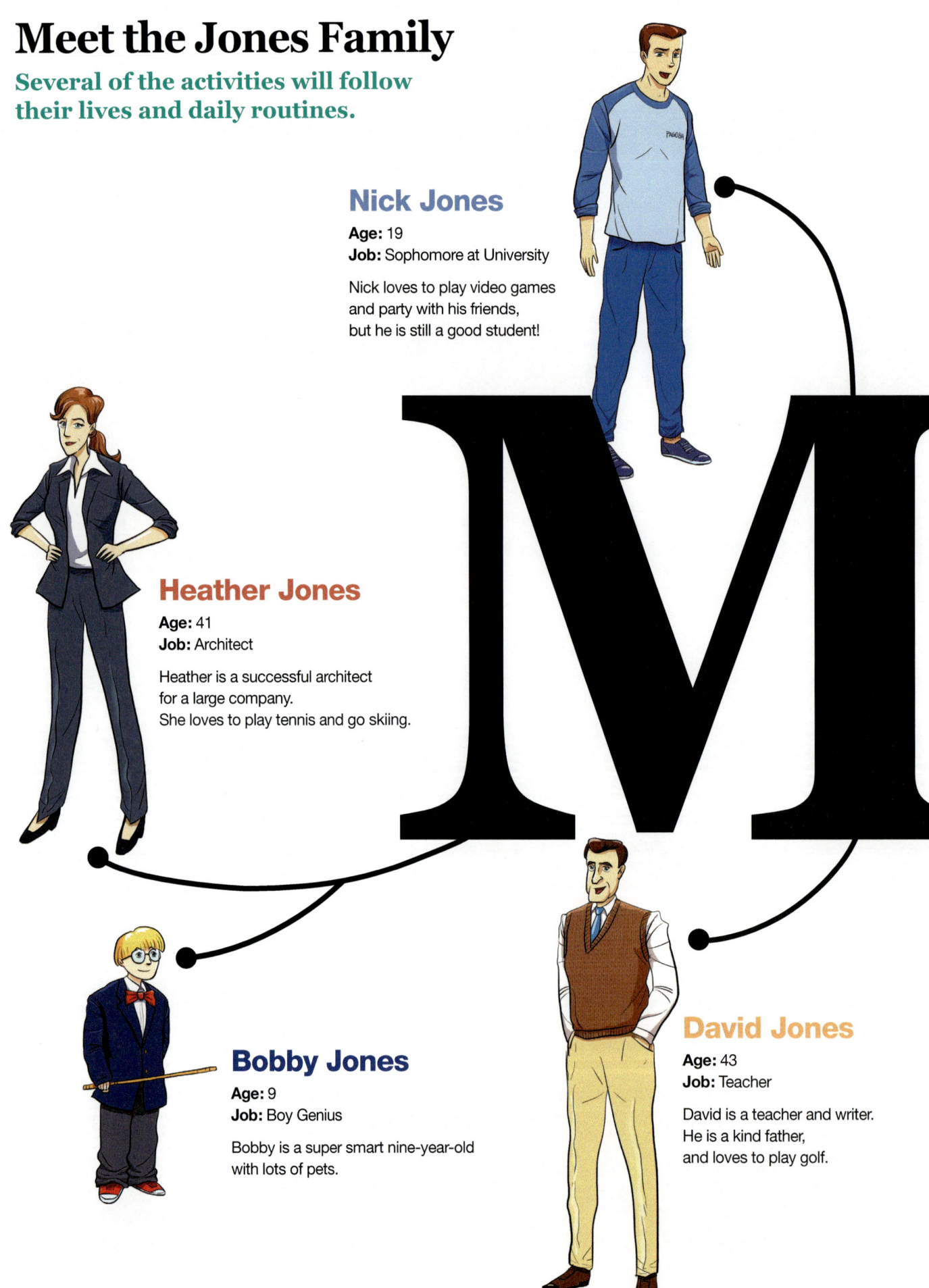

01
Don't I Know You?
Introductions & Reporting

Objectives:
/ Practice asking for additional information
/ Listen to dialogue about proverbs and expressions

WARM UP

PART 1

Brainstorm questions related to the following topics:
- Name
- School/Work
- Age
- Hobby
- Home

PART 2

- Ask your partner the questions you brainstormed in part 1.

TONGUE TWISTERS

- She said she should sit, so she sat.

LESSON 1

A. Questions & Clarifications

Language Point : Ask Questions

Asking questions is an important part of becoming a better speaker.

PART 1

1. Which of these things did you learn without help?
    a. How to tie your shoe.
    b. How to play an **instrument**.
    c. Advanced mathematics.

2. What happens if you don't ask questions?
    a. You magically gain the knowledge anyway.
    b. You continue doing it wrong.
    c. Your teacher will think you know everything.

3. How should you respond to a question?
    a. **Panic** and run away.
    b. Stare at the person.
    c. **Giggle** like a young child.

4. Why is it important to ask follow-up questions?
    a. To **annoy** the person you are talking to.
    b. To hear yourself talk.
    c. To show that you understand and are listening.

When we want to improve, we need to ask questions.

If you don't ask questions, you might waste the time you've spent in class!

Just asking one question is usually not enough!

Always give some kind of answer, even if you've never thought about it before.

Instrument (*n.*): object that makes music
Panic (*v.*): to suddenly feel fear
Giggle (*v.*): to laugh quickly
Annoy (*v.*): to make someone feel a little angry

PART 2

> Ask your partner the question.
> Then ask at least two follow-up questions related to the topic.

Fashion and Shopping
What do you like to shop for?

Talent and Ability
What are you good at?

Film and Media
What was the last movie you saw?

Animals and Pets
Do you have a pet?

Food and Cooking
What can you cook?

Family
Where does your family live?

Celebrities
Who is your favorite actor/singer?

Occupations
Where do you work/go to school?

Sports and Hobbies
How do you spend your free time?

Travel and Plans
When was your last trip?

Books and Stories
Do you like reading?

Romance and Relationships
Are you involved with anyone?

Unit 1 Don't I Know You? | 13

B. What Does That Mean?

Language Point : Asking For More Information

Part of being a good conversation partner is asking follow-up questions. Follow-up questions are very helpful if you don't completely understand what someone has said.

- Did you say _____? What's that?
- What is/are _____?
- What does _____ mean?

Tip: Be specific

It is important to be specific about what you don't understand instead of just saying, "I don't understand."

Example:

Teacher, I don't understand. (not specific)
Teacher, what does the word "flirt" mean? (specific)

Pre-listening

> Are you **curious** about your teacher?
> Take turns asking your teacher the questions below.
> Ask a follow-up question even if you know the answer.

1. What's your full name?
   - What does _____ mean?

2. Where are you from?
   - Did you say _____? Where's that?

3. What is your favorite kind of music?
   - I'm sorry, what is _____?

4. What is your blood type?
   - _____?

Listening TRACK 2-3

David is discussing an assignment with his student Daniel. Select the correct explanation they give for the expressions below.

That's the bomb!
A. That's good!
B. That's bad.

More than one way to skin a cat
A. There is no way to solve the problem.
B. There are different ways to solve the problem.

Post-listening

With a partner, ask each other the meaning of the following **proverbs**.

> **Example:**
> **A:** What does *take it one step at a time* mean?
> **B:** It's probably A. It means *be careful and don't hurry*.

Proverbs

① TAKE IT ONE STEP AT A TIME.

② PRACTICE MAKES PERFECT.

③ WHAT'S DONE IS DONE.

④ TOMORROW IS A NEW DAY.

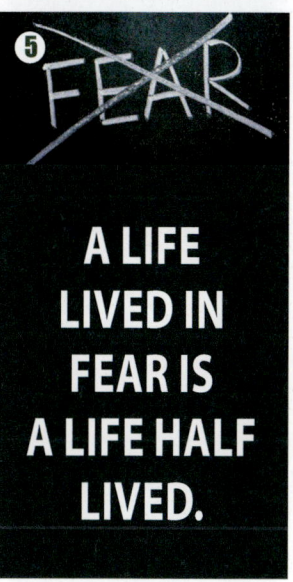

⑤ A LIFE LIVED IN FEAR IS A LIFE HALF LIVED.

Meanings

A Be careful, and don't hurry.
B If you want to be good at something, you need to do it often.
C Don't worry about a mistake. You can't change it.
D You can always have another chance.
E You can't be successful unless you try.

Flirt (v.): to show interest in or attraction to someone
Curious (adj.): want to know something
Proverb (n.): a well-known saying that expresses truth

C. Don't I Know You?

Did you meet your partner somewhere before?
> Take turns reading the questions and answering them.
> Ask your partner what he/she means by his/her answer. You don't have to use the pictures.

Example: Food

A: *Did you say you like greasy food?*
B: *Actually, I prefer pricey food.*
A: *What do you mean by pricey food?*
B: *I enjoy going out for food like oysters, lobster, and steak.*

1. FOOD
Did you say you like **greasy food**?
A. Pricey food
B. Fast food
C. Mom's food

2. INTERESTS
You said you really liked American Football, right?

A. Baseball
B. Video games
C. Board games

3. PETS
You said you had a cat in elementary school?
A. A dog
B. A bird
C. A frog

4. MOVIES
Did you say you like really old movies?
A. Romantic comedies
B. Horror movies
C. Action movies

5. TRAVEL
Did you say you're going to the mall next weekend?
A. To the ocean
B. To the mountains
C. To a club

Greasy (*adj.*): oily to the touch
Pricey (*adj.*): costing a lot of money

Discussion **Questions**

1. Why are you taking this class?

   ▶ What are some good ways to improve your speaking?

2. Do you prefer having discussions in a group or do you like one-to-one conversations?

   ▶ Who do you usually have long conversations with?

3. Do you feel comfortable or scared asking someone a question when you don't know the answer?

   ▶ When is it bad to ask questions?

4. How much time do you spend studying English every day?

   ▶ How much time should you study English every day if you want to improve?

5. What do you do when you don't understand something in English?

   ▶ What could you do differently?

6. Which of these topics are okay to ask people about in your country? Which ones are not okay?

LESSON 2

>> WARM UP

Objectives:
/ Talk about what was previously said
/ Make guesses about what others said

Match the famous **quote** to the person who said it.

Santa

Martin Luther King Jr.

Hamlet

Who said,
1. "I'll be back."?
2. "To be, or not to be, that is the question."?
3. "I have a dream…"?
4. "Ho, Ho, Ho. Merry Christmas!"?
5. "One small step for a man. One giant leap for mankind."?

Neil Armstrong

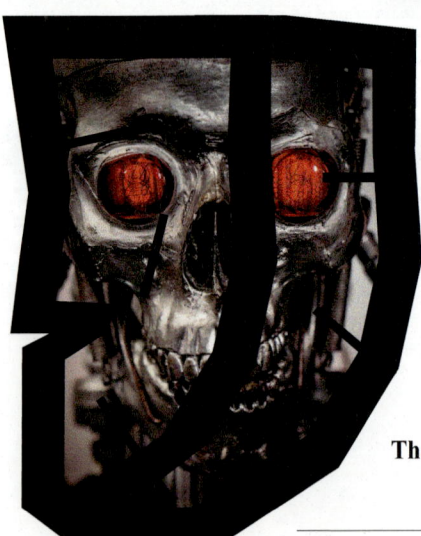

The Terminator

Quote (*n.*): the exact words spoken by someone

A. Can I See Your Pictures?

PART 1

Imagine that the photo below is of your family. With a partner, answer the following questions.

1. What are your parents' or grandparents' names?
2. How many brothers and sisters do you have?
   - What are their names?
   - Are they older or younger?
3. Where does your family live?
4. Where was the last place you went on vacation together?
5. When was the last time you took a family photo?

Language Point : Asking About What Was Said

Look at the conversation between Jack and Jill.
▸ Jill uses the verb "say" to find out information about things she didn't hear.
▸ Notice how the words are not exactly the same.

Jon
-Hey! I went on a trip to New York.
-No, not for work. I went with my sister to a family reunion.
-Not tonight. I feel tired. I want to just stay at home.

What did Jon say on the phone?
Where did he say he went?
Who did he say he went with?
So, does he want to join us?

He said he went on a trip to New York.
He said he went with his sister for a family reunion.
He says he's tired and wants to stay in.

PART 2

Now work with a different partner. Tell them what your previous partner said about the family photo in part 1.

1. What are his/her parents' names? *He/she said their names are*...
2. How many brothers and sisters does he/she have?
   He/she said he/she has...
   • What are their names? *He/she said their names are*...
   • Are they older or younger? *He/she said they are*...
3. Where did he/she say they lived?
4. Where did he/she say they went on vacation last?
5. When did he/she say the last time they took a photo was?

PART 3

> Share some photos of your friends or family with your partner.
> Now go around the class in a circle and show everyone your picture.
> The person you were just talking to should tell everyone what you said about the person in the picture.

B. Comic Gap Fill

Use the pictures and prompts to tell the story with your partner.

two friends talking

an older woman at a cafe'

a married couple hiking

tourists asking a local for help

an astronaut on the moon

C. He Said, She Said

PART 1 • Interview your partner about his/her life. After each question, ask a follow-up question.

Past
1. What did you do last weekend?
2. Where were you yesterday at noon?
3. What was the last movie you saw?
4. How long did you sleep last night?

Present
1. What's your full name?
2. Do you like listening to music?
3. How many people live in your house?
4. What kind of phone do you have?

Future
1. Will you ever be rich and famous?
2. What are you going to do on your next vacation?
3. What will the weather be like tomorrow?
4. When are you going home tonight?

Example:
A: *What's your full name?*
B: *My name is Leeroy. My family name is Jenkins.*
A: *Where did you get your name?*
B: *It was my father's name!*

PART 2

> Divide the class into two teams. The person you interviewed should be on the opposite team.
> Your teacher will be the "host". When it is your turn, choose a category.
> The host will ask you what your partner said.
> You must report what your partner said and what he/she said to your follow-up question.
> If you are wrong, your old partner can "steal" the category. Once a category is answered correctly, it cannot be chosen again.

> **Example:**
>
> **A:** *I want "Yesterday at Noon" for 200 points.*
> **Host:** *Where did your partner say he was yesterday at noon?*
> **A:** *He said he was at home. He said he was watching TV with his sister.*
> **Host:** *Is that true?*
> **B:** *Yes, that is what I said.*

Past

Last Weekend — Points: 100

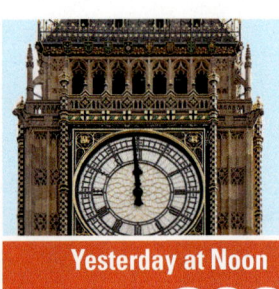
Yesterday at Noon — Points: 200

Last Movie — Points: 300

Last Night — Points: 400

Present

Full Name — Points: 100

Music — Points: 200

Phone — Points: 300

In the House — Points: 400

Future

Go Home — Points: 100

Next Vacation — Points: 200

Rich and Famous — Points: 300

Tomorrow's Weather — Points: 400

Discussion
Questions

1. What is something your parents said to you a lot when you were young?
   - Do you follow their advice?

2. What is something you heard recently on the news?
   - What do you think about it?

3. When was the last time someone said something _____ to you?
   - Funny
   - Strange
   - Mean
   - Kind

4. What did the weather report say the weather is going to be like tomorrow?
   - Do you think the weather report is **accurate** in your city?

5. Are you good or bad at telling jokes?
   - Who do you think says funny things a lot on TV?

6. When someone is lying to you, are you good at noticing?
   - What is something people say or do when lying?

7. What is something a famous person said that has **influenced** you?
   - What would you say to a famous dead person if you could meet him or her?

UNIT 1 REVIEW

How well can you use…
- ☐ Expressions for asking about additional information?
- ☐ Ways to report what other people have said?

What do you need to study more?

Accurate *(adj.)*: free from any error
Influenced *(adj.)*: power to affect thinking

Activity: The Wise Man

Your partner met a wise man while traveling. Ask your partner what the wise man said.

1. What did he say you should do before you leap?
2. What did he say too many cooks do?
3. What did he say things that don't kill you do?
4. What did he say every cloud has?
5. Where did he say you shouldn't put your eggs?
6. What animal did he say can be skinned in many ways?

A. Too many cooks spoil the *broth*.

B. Don't put all your eggs in one *basket*.

C. There are many ways to skin a cat.

D. Every cloud has a *silver lining*.

E. What doesn't kill you makes you stronger.

F. Look before you *leap*.

"The wise man said,"

Now ask your partner:
- What does _____ mean?
- I think it means _____.

1 Meaning: *Carefully plan things before you start. If you don't have a good plan, you might fail.*

2 Meaning: *If too many people are trying to do something, it will fail. It's better to have one person directing a project than many people.*

3 Meaning: *There is a positive side to every bad situation. Bad things can also produce some good results.*

4 Meaning: *Do not depend on one thing for success. Don't put all your money in one place because you might lose everything if it fails.*

5 Meaning: *You become stronger when bad things happen to you. If someone cheats you out of money, you won't make the mistake again.*

6 Meaning: *There is more than one way to solve a problem. If one solution doesn't work, try to find another way to solve the problem.*

Broth (*n.*): clear soup
Basket (*n.*): a container made of woven strips
Silver Lining (*n.*): something that offers hope
Leap (*v.*): big jump
Depend (*v.*): to need someone or something
Cheat (*v.*): to lie to or mislead someone for personal gain

 **David:**
I had an interesting conversation with one of my students today. It was the bomb!

 David: I had an interesting conversation with one of my students today. It was the bomb!

 Ella: Dad, you REALLY can't use that expression!

 David: Why not?

 Ella: It's so old…and I think you are too old to use that kind of slang anyway. It's not cool!! What if my friends read this?

 David: Aw, come on Ella, take a chill pill!

 Ella: A what?

 Heather He means relax, Ella.

 David: That's another cool expression!

 Ella: Maybe it was cool in the 80's…

 Heather Too cool for school.

 Ella: Stop it!!

A. Discussion
1. What are some expressions in your native language that are no longer said?
2. What are some expressions that young people can say, but old people can't? Are there expressions that old people can say, but young people can't?

B. Writing
Write three questions for your teacher about words or phrases you don't understand in English.

02
Wish You Were Here
Opinions & Suggestions

Objectives:
/ Ask for and give opinions about travel
/ Listen to a story of someone's trip

WARM UP

For vacations, which is better?
Why do you think so?

Backpack vs. Suitcase

Winter vs. Summer

Country vs. City

Hotel vs. Hostel

Sightseeing vs. Shopping

LESSON 1

A. You've Got a Point There

Language Point : Asking What Others Think

Do you think...?
Do you think people like visiting your country?
-Yes. I think tourists really like it here.

What do you think about....?
What do you think about tourists in your country?
I think tourists are annoying.

Why do you think...?
Why do you think tourists are annoying?
I think they're annoying because they expect everyone to speak their language.

Tip
You can make your opinion sound stronger by stressing words like *really* and *very*.
I think it's very important.

Ask your partner the first question. Answer the question with your opinion. Ask the "thumbs up" question if your partner thinks it's good. Ask the "thumbs down" question if your partner thinks it's bad.

1. What do you think about **package tours**?
   👍 Why do you think they are good?
   👎 Why do you think they are bad?

2. What do you think about eating the local food?
   👍 Why do you think it's good?
   👎 Why do you think it's bad?

3. Do you think it's important to visit famous places?
   👍 Why do you think it's important?
   👎 Why don't you think it's important?

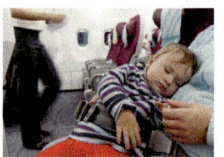
4. Do you think flying is the best way to travel?
   👍 Why do you think flying is good?
   👎 Why do you think flying is bad?

5. What do you think about traveling alone?
   👍 Why do you like traveling alone?
   👎 Why don't you like traveling alone?

Package tour (*n.*): a travel tour which includes everything

B. Wish You Were Here

Pre-listening

Look at the postcards below. What do you think about each place?
Which vacation destinations do you want to visit?
Which ones don't you want to visit? Why?

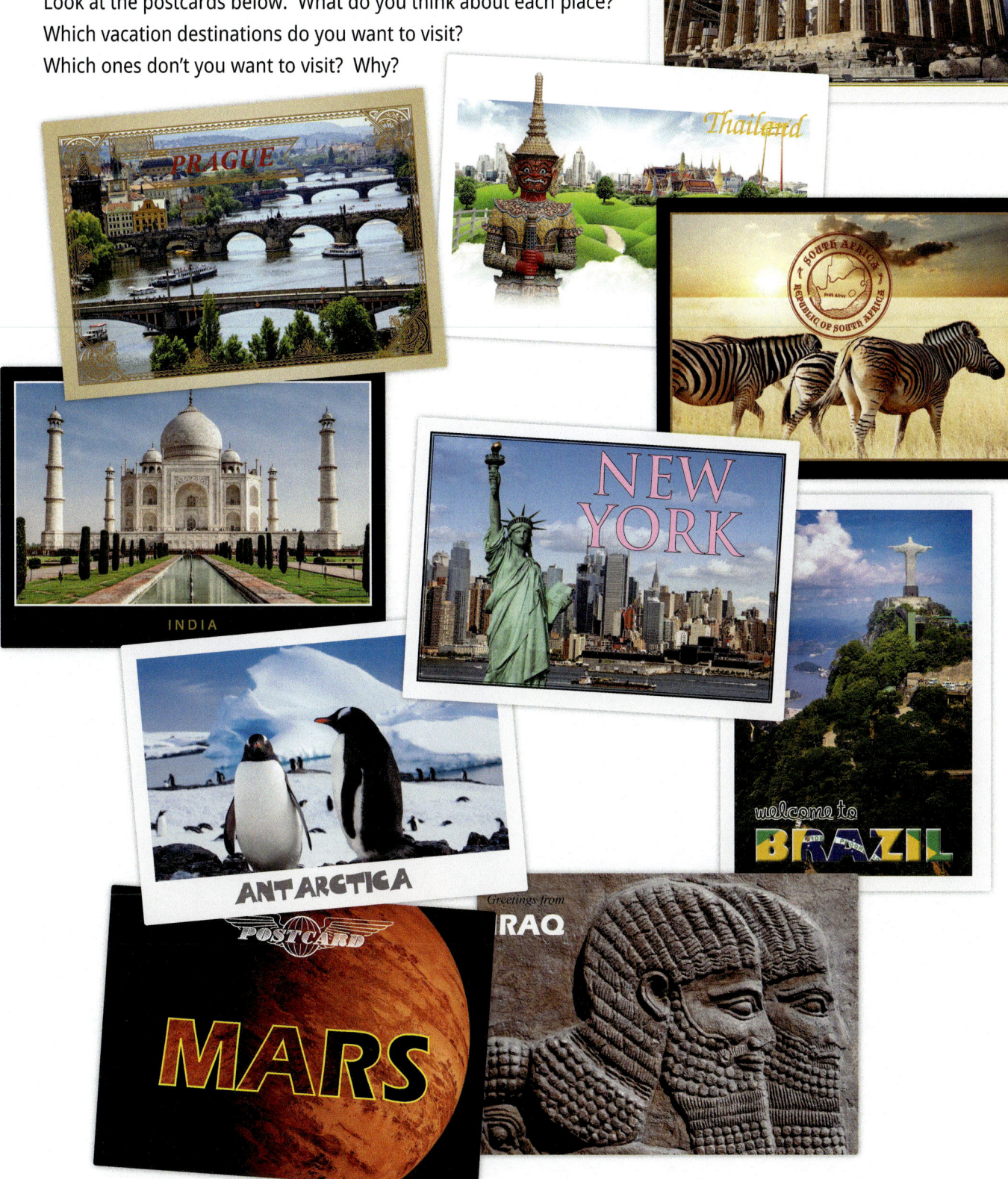

Listening  TRACK 4-5

1. Look at the images below and guess which things you think Grandma Ruth is doing on her vacation.
2. Check the box related to the activity that Grandma Ruth did on her vacation to the nation of Kipi Kipi.

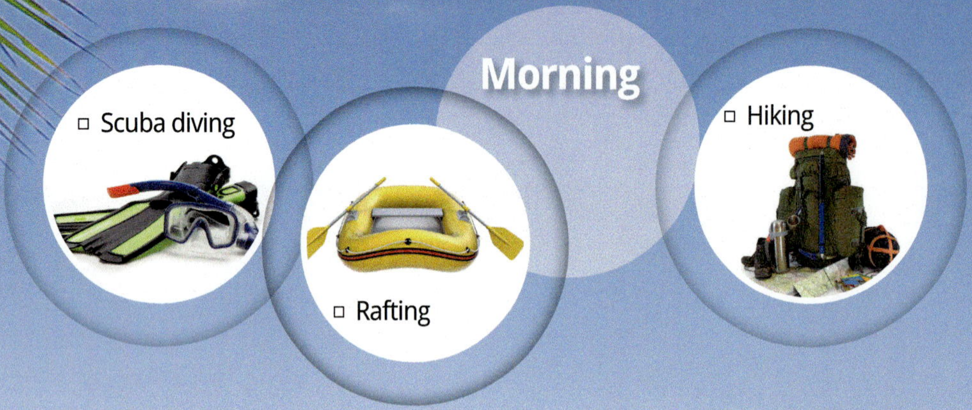

Morning
- ☐ Scuba diving
- ☐ Rafting
- ☐ Hiking

Lunch
- ☐ Fruit
- ☐ Chicken
- ☐ Fish

Souvenir
- ☐ Tattoo
- ☐ Wine
- ☐ Keychain

Problem
- ☐ Theft
- ☐ Food poisoning
- ☐ Jail

Sightseeing (*n.*): visiting places of interest
Food poisoning (*n.*): sickness from eating bad food

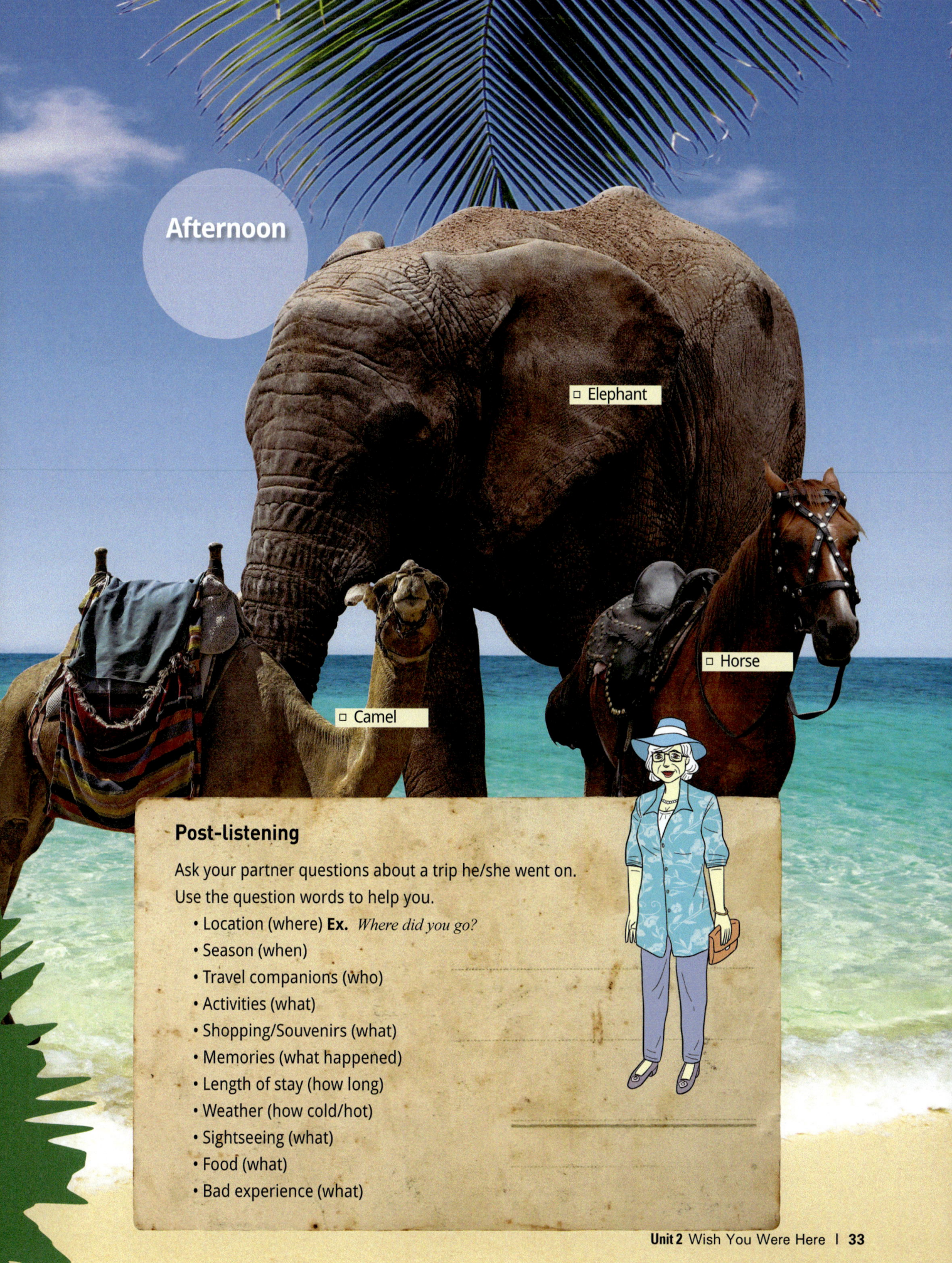

Afternoon

- Elephant
- Camel
- Horse

Post-listening

Ask your partner questions about a trip he/she went on. Use the question words to help you.
- Location (where) **Ex.** *Where did you go?*
- Season (when)
- Travel companions (who)
- Activities (what)
- Shopping/Souvenirs (what)
- Memories (what happened)
- Length of stay (how long)
- Weather (how cold/hot)
- Sightseeing (what)
- Food (what)
- Bad experience (what)

C. Easy Peasy Postcard Generator

PART 1

Think of a trip you took in the past or **make one up** (it doesn't have to be real). Circle each choice and think of some reasons for each choice.

1. Hey _____! I'm having a **marvelous/ awful** time in _____.

2. The weather is...

Good ☐   Not bad ☐   Terrible ☐

3. The journey here was...

Incredible ☐   Annoying ☐   Horrible ☐

4. The hotel room is...

Luxurious ☐   Uncomfortable ☐   Shocking ☐

5. Yesterday, dinner was...

Tasty ☐   Greasy ☐   Nasty ☐

6. The local people are...

Interesting ☐   Boring ☐   Strange ☐

Yours Truly, _____

PART 2

Now, look at your partner's postcard. Ask follow-up questions to find out more information.

1 When did you go to _____?

2 Why did you say the weather was _____?
  • What things did you do?
  • (Another question) _____?

3 Why was the journey there so _____?
  • How long did it take you to get there?
  • (Another question) _____?

4 Why did you say the room was _____?
  • How many nights did you sleep there?
  • (Another question) _____?

5 Why was dinner _____?
  • What other things did you try?
  • (Another question) _____?

6 Why did you say the people were _____?
  • Who did you meet?
  • (Another question) _____?

Discussion Questions

1. When was the last time you flew?
   - Where did you go?

2. Do you like taking the train?
   - How often do you take a train?

3. What is your favorite airline?
   - Did you ever fly first class?

4. Do you prefer to take a train or an airplane on a long trip? Why?

5. Have you ever slept on an overnight train?
   - When?
   - Where?
   - What was it like?

6. Have you ever missed a plane or train?
   - Why?
   - What did you do?

7. Have you ever taken a cruise before?
   - What was it like?

LESSON 2

>> WARM UP

Objectives:
/ Practice making friendly suggestions
/ Make definite suggestions based on opinion

Lost in Transit

Where have these suitcases been? What kinds of souvenirs have you brought back from your travels?

A. Let's Go!

Language Point : Making Suggestions

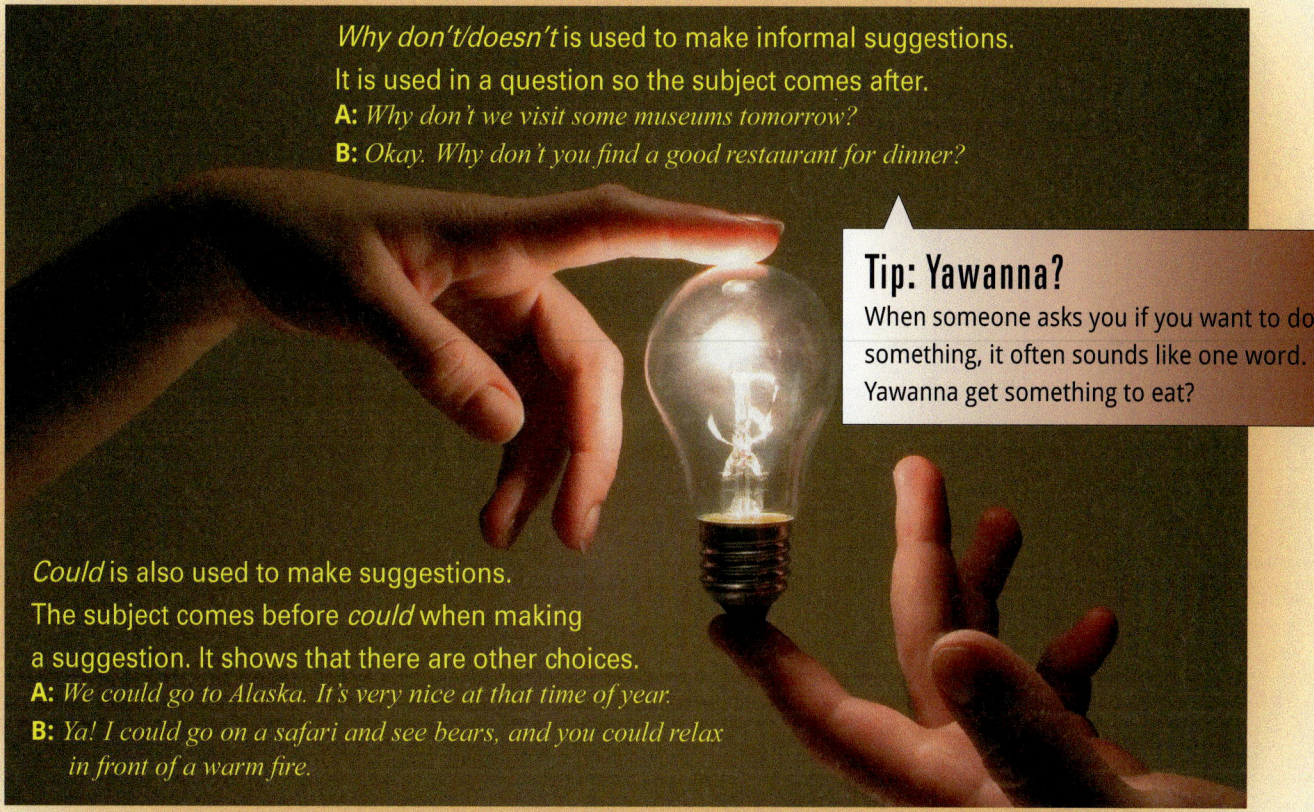

Why don't/doesn't is used to make informal suggestions.
It is used in a question so the subject comes after.
A: *Why don't we visit some museums tomorrow?*
B: *Okay. Why don't you find a good restaurant for dinner?*

Tip: Yawanna?
When someone asks you if you want to do something, it often sounds like one word. Yawanna get something to eat?

Could is also used to make suggestions. The subject comes before *could* when making a suggestion. It shows that there are other choices.
A: *We could go to Alaska. It's very nice at that time of year.*
B: *Ya! I could go on a safari and see bears, and you could relax in front of a warm fire.*

PART 1 ● Practice the dialogue below with a partner. Use why don't we or we could, and come up with a plan.

A: I'm hungry. Do you want to get something to eat?
B: Sure. Where do you want to go?
A: We could go to _____ (restaurant) _____.
B: Sounds good.
A: What time do you want to meet?
B: Why don't we meet at _____ (time) _____?
A: Okay. Let's meet at _____.
B: What do you want to do after we eat?
A: We could _____ (activity) _____ or _____ (activity) _____.
B: _____ sounds good.
A: Who can we ask to join us?
B: Why don't we ask _____?

Unit 2 Wish You Were Here | 39

PART 2 ● The people below need some suggestions for their vacations. What are some things they could do on their trips?

1. Irene and Isaac are in Italy.

Why don't they _____?

2. Nicky is in Egypt.

She could _____

3. Carl and Candace are in Canada.

They could _____, or they could ____

4. Brad and Brandi are in Brazil.

Why don't they _____?

5. The Nelsons are in New Zealand.

_____
_____

6. Tabitha is in Thailand.
Why doesn't she _____?

B. Ecotourism

Language Point: Could vs. Should

Could is used to make suggestions and give possibilities.
You could try the tacos or the lobster. They're both delicious.

Should is used when you want to make a more definite suggestion or give advice.
You should try the tacos. They're the best.

PART 1

> Look at the Rules of the Traveler.
> Do you agree with these rules?
> What are some other important things to think about when traveling?

RULES OF THE TRAVELER:

1. We should travel so we can learn.
2. We should respect the local culture.
3. We shouldn't waste **resources**.
4. We should leave an area like we found it.
5. We should be **flexible** and **patient**.

PART 2

Look at the situations on the next page.
> Which of the Rules of the Traveler apply to each situation?
> Do you think the rule should apply, or are their actions okay in that situation?

Example: There was a big party on the beach.

Student A: *This is Rule #4! They should clean up after a party.*
Student B: *Yeah, I don't want to go to that beach now.*
Student A: *It could also be bad for the local animals.*
Student B: *Did you ever go to a beach party?*

Resources (*n.*): environmental assets such as water and energy
Flexible (*adj.*): able to change to a new situation
Patient (*adj.*): able to endure waiting

EC⦰ TOURISM

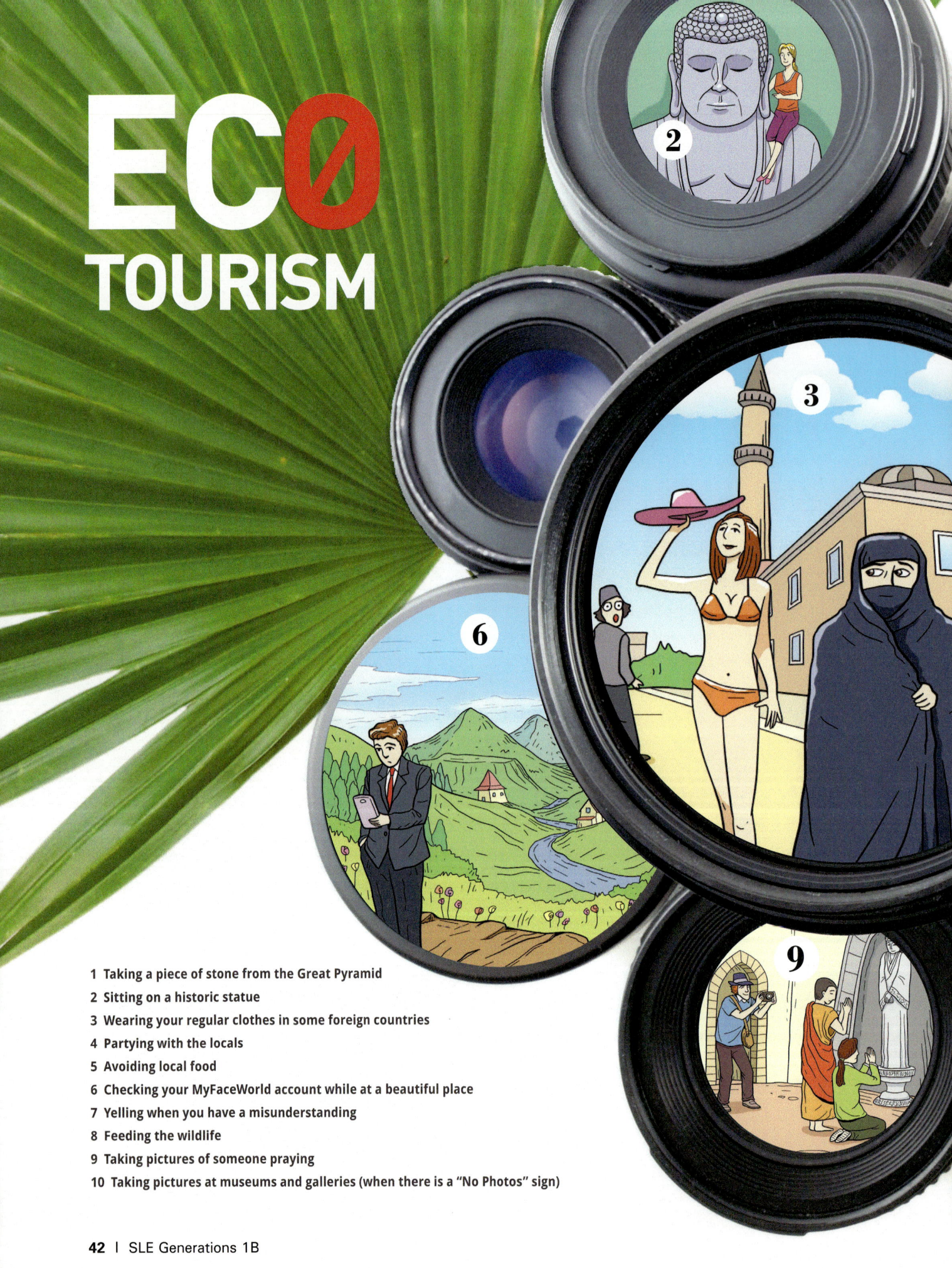

1 Taking a piece of stone from the Great Pyramid
2 Sitting on a historic statue
3 Wearing your regular clothes in some foreign countries
4 Partying with the locals
5 Avoiding local food
6 Checking your MyFaceWorld account while at a beautiful place
7 Yelling when you have a misunderstanding
8 Feeding the wildlife
9 Taking pictures of someone praying
10 Taking pictures at museums and galleries (when there is a "No Photos" sign)

C. EntertainU World Travel Agency

PART 1
Look at the following theme vacations with a partner, and discuss which ones you like and why.

SPOOKY CENTRAL
- Here, It's Always Halloween

You'll be scared NOT to have fun.

Lodging
Haunted House

Food
Spooky food

Activity 1
The Haunted Rollercoaster

Activity 2
Zombie Tag

Lover's Lane
- Fall in Love All Over Again -

Whether its your honeymoon, or a chance to take relationship-building games and courses, you'll fall in love all over again when you take a walk down Lover's Lane.

Lodging	Private beach hut
Food	Couples Kitchen
Activity 1	Love boats
Activity 2	Relationship classes

- Next Stop

single's shelter

Don't you hate going to parks and seeing all of those annoying couples? Don't worry, everyone here is on the menu!

Lodging	Bunk-bed group rooms
Food	Family-style buffet
Activity 1	Speed-dating
Activity 2	Mixer/bar crawl

Golden Paradise
– Where Everything is Gold!

Weren't born a king? Now you can see what it's like!

Lodging   Golden Palace
Food   Personal chef
Activity 1 Fine wine tasting
Activity 2 The Opera

The Leaf

– Health, Fitness, Green, Nature, etc.

Don't vacation for yourself – vacation for the planet.

Lodging: Tree house
Food: Organic food
Activity 1: Yoga
Activity 2: Healthy cooking class

Lady Lake

Man Cave AND Lady Lake
When You Need a Break

SOMETIMES YOU'VE JUST GOT TO GET AWAY FROM THE OPPOSITE SEX.

Lodging
Home theater basement / Tea house
Food
Meat and beer / Salads and tea
Activity 1
Sports / Spa
Activity 2
Video game competition / Shopping

Man Cave

PART 2 • Travel Agency to the Not Quite Stars

You and your partner work for EntertainU World Travel Agency. The following groups want you to plan their vacation. Where will you send each group? You can't send two groups to the same place.

2. The Retirees
2 grandparents
Someplace quiet and relaxing

1. The Young Teens
2 guys / 2 girls
Just want to have fun

5. Extended-Family Tour
3 grandparents
6 parents
4 teens
Something for everyone

3. The Lone Wolf
1 person
Seeking adventure

4. The Married With Crying Child Couple
A man, a woman, and their baby
Family friendly fun time

6. The Honeymooners
A newly married man and woman

Discussion Questions

1. Have you ever been to an amusement park?
   - Which one?
   - What was it like?
   - What's your favorite amusement park?

2. What are some popular places for tourists to visit in your city?
   - In your country?

3. What place do people like to go to on vacation that you don't like? Why?

4. Do you have any future travel plans?
   - Where do you want to go?
   - When?
   - Who do you want to go with?

5. What are some things you have to do before going on a trip?

6. What are some things you should do when traveling to be safe?

UNIT 2 REVIEW

How well can you use…
- ☐ Language for asking and giving opinions?
- ☐ Friendly and definite suggestions?

What do you need to study more?

Activity: World Traveler

Work with a partner to fill in as many of the words as you know. Then, work with another team to see if you can fill in what's missing.

What country's flag is this? | **What do you call someone from...?** | **What language(s) do they speak?**

- 🇨🇦 Canada — _____ — English/_____
- 🇵🇭 _____ — Filipino — _____
- 🇪🇸 _____ — Spaniard — _____
- 🇩🇪 _____ — German — _____
- 🇦🇺 Australia — _____ — _____
- 🇨🇿 Czech Republic — _____ — _____
- 🇿🇦 _____ — South African — _____
- 🇧🇷 _____ — _____ — Portuguese
- 🇨🇭 Switzerland — _____ — _____
- 🇨🇳 _____ — _____ — Mandarin/_____

ALBUM TITLE: KIPI KIPI VACATION PICS

Posted By: Ruth   **Segue**

This was where I stayed after our little adventure. It was actually very comfortable, and the food was free! I met lots of new and interesting people here.

Location:
Kipi Kipi

My scuba instructor, Hannah! In this picture, she says that I am doing very well! Or maybe that I have three minutes of air left. I don't remember.

Location:
Kipi Kipi

Earl, my new favorite elephant! This picture was before we went on our little adventure...

Location:
Kipi Kipi

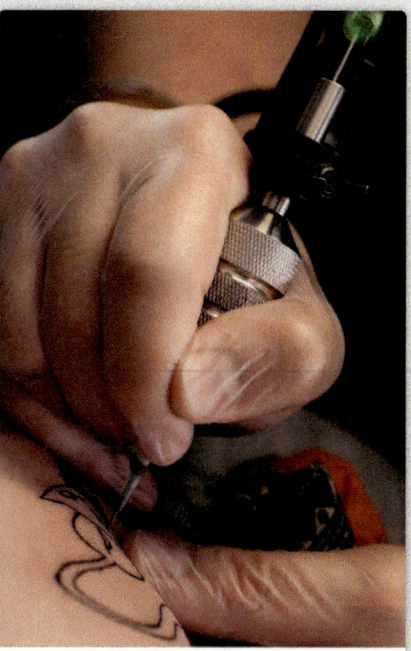

I made a new friend in jail. His name is Spider and he is an artist! He drew a picture on me for free. It was so exciting. I hope it washes off soon...

Location:
Kipi Kipi

A. Discussion
1. Do you think Grandma Ruth's trip was fun or boring?
2. Have you met interesting people while traveling? Who were they?

B. Writing
Choose a few of your own pictures and write captions for them!

Unit 2 Wish You Were Here | 49

03
The Human Environment
Comparisons & Homes

Objectives:
/ Use comparison language
/ Listen to a story about comparing apartments

WARM UP

Describe your bedroom.

- What furniture do you have in your room?
- Do you have a window? What can you see from the window?
- What do you have on the walls?
- How much time do you spend in your room?
- What do you want to change about it?

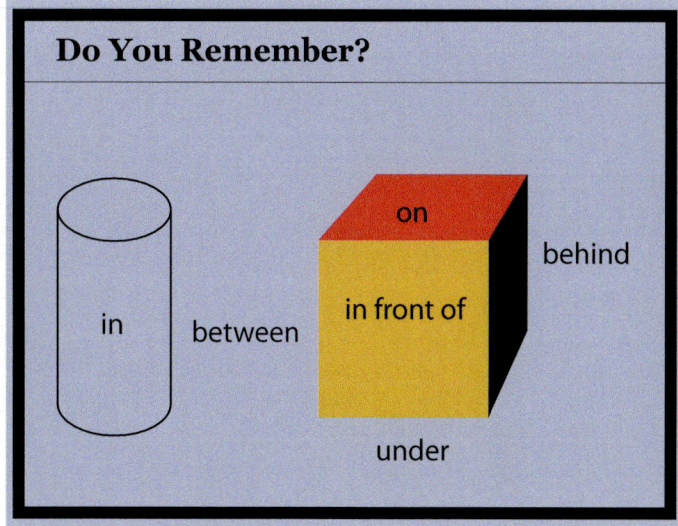

Do You Remember?

in, between, on, in front of, behind, under

Unit 3 The Human Environment | 51

LESSON 1

A. Where Are My Keys?

You can't find several items in your house. Ask your partner if he/she knows where the items are in the house.

Example: Hat

A: *Do you know where my hat is?*
B: *Uh, I don't see it. What does it look like?*
A: *It's a black hat. It looks very formal.*
B: *Ah, it's on the bed in the bedroom.*
A: *Which bedroom?*
B: *The bedroom with the computer in it.*
A: *Great. Thanks!*

Student A needs to find:

- Shoe
- Cat
- Sandwich
- Love
- Tools
- Remote control
- Backpack
- Hat

52 | SLE Generations 1B

Student B needs to find:

Book · Keys · Teddy bear · Baby · Phone · Drink · DVD · Jacket

Example: Hat

A: *Do you know where my hat is?*
B: *Uh, I don't see it. What does it look like?*
A: *It's a black hat. It looks very formal.*
B: *Ah, it's on the bed in the bedroom.*
A: *Which bedroom?*
B: *The bedroom with the computer in it.*
A: *Great. Thanks!*

Unit 3 The Human Environment | 53

B. Mine's Bigger

Language Point : Comparatives & Superlatives

Comparatives show the difference between *this* and *that*.

This house is *bigger than* that house.	*-er + than* for one-syllable words
This house is *more expensive than* that one.	*more + than* for two-syllable words
This house is *uglier than* that house.	*-ier + than* for words that end in -y
This house is *better/worse/farther than* that one.	*good, bad,* and *far* are exceptions

Pre-listening

Use the words in the box (and any others you can think of) to make comparisons of the things below.

| Big | Small | Boring | Exciting | Expensive | Cheap | Fast | Slow |
| Crowded | Empty | Relaxing | Stressful | Safe | Dangerous | Quiet | Loud |

1. a house / an apartment

2. a park / a shopping mall

> **Ex:** **A:** *I think a house is quieter than an apartment.*
> **B:** *But an apartment is safer than a house.*
> **A:** *Why do you think so?*

3. a bus / the subway

4. taking a trip / staying at home

5. museums / stadiums

6. fast food / home cooked food

7. going to the dentist / going to the doctor

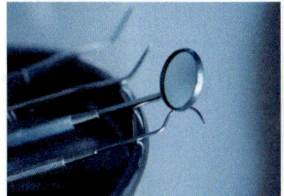 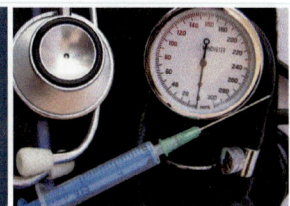

8. a swimming pool / the gym

Listening TRACK 6-7

Ella just graduated and is searching for an apartment. Listen to Ella and her Dad compare the two apartments.

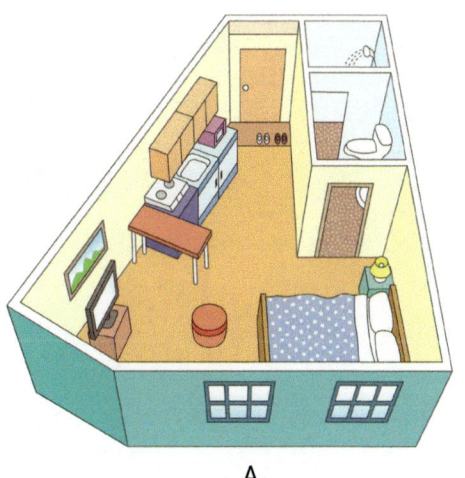
A

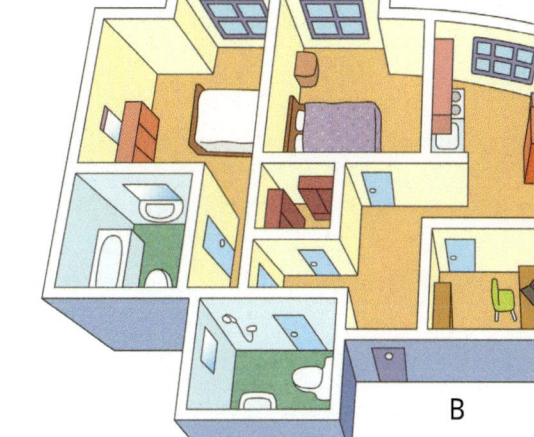
B

	Price	Space	Location
Apartment A	cheap/expensive	spacious/cozy	close/far
Apartment B	cheap/expensive	spacious/cozy	close/far

Unit 3 The Human Environment | 55

Post-listening

Superlatives compare one part of a group to the whole group.

This house is *the biggest*.	*the* + *-est* for one-syllable words
That house is *the most expensive*.	*the* + *most* for two-syllable words
This house is *the ugliest*.	*the* + *-iest* for words that end in -y
This house is the *best/worst/farthest*.	*good, bad, and far* are exceptions

◇ Note: A prepositional phrase (*of all time, in the world, on TV*) is often added to a superlative.

Discuss the following pictures in groups.

1. How are the eggs different?

2. How are the dogs different?

3. How are the homes different?

4. How are the sandwiches different?

5. How are the cars different?

Comparative Blackjack

PART 2
- Write three questions of your own to make "cards", and play as a class.
- Give point values for the most, the least, and the middle position.
- Put your points in the chips at the bottom.

BlackJack pays 3 to 2
Play in groups of three or more
Closest to 21 wins

Question 1
How...

__ points=

__ points=

__ point=

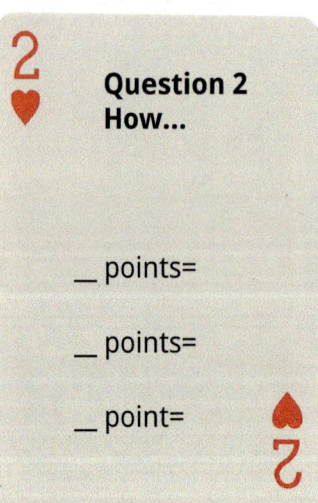

Question 2
How...

__ points=

__ points=

__ point=

Question 3
How...

__ points=

__ points=

__ point=

Points

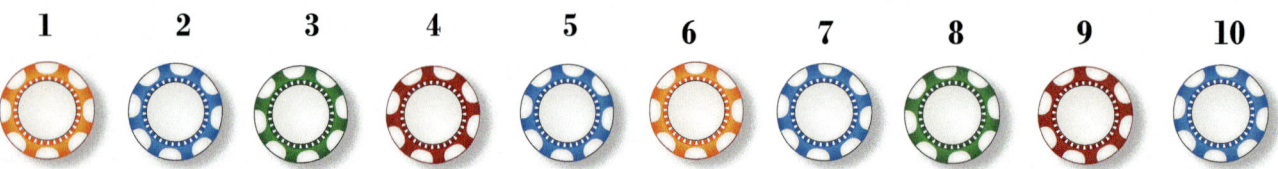

1 2 3 4 5 6 7 8 9 10

Discussion Questions

1. Which area of the city do you live in?
   - How can you compare it to other areas of the city?

2. How many **neighborhoods** have you lived in?
   - How are they different?

3. How are some of the other cities in your country different?
   - How about cities in other countries?

4. How many of your neighbors do you know?
   - Can you compare them? Who's friendlier, younger, etc.?

5. How has your life changed since you graduated from high school?
   - How are high school and university different?

6. Who do you live with?
   - Do you want to live with more or fewer people? Why?

7. How many cars has your family owned?
   - Which one was the best? Why?

Neighborhood (n.): the general area of a place

LESSON 2

>> WARM UP

Objectives:
/ Describe distance
/ Talk about differences and similarities

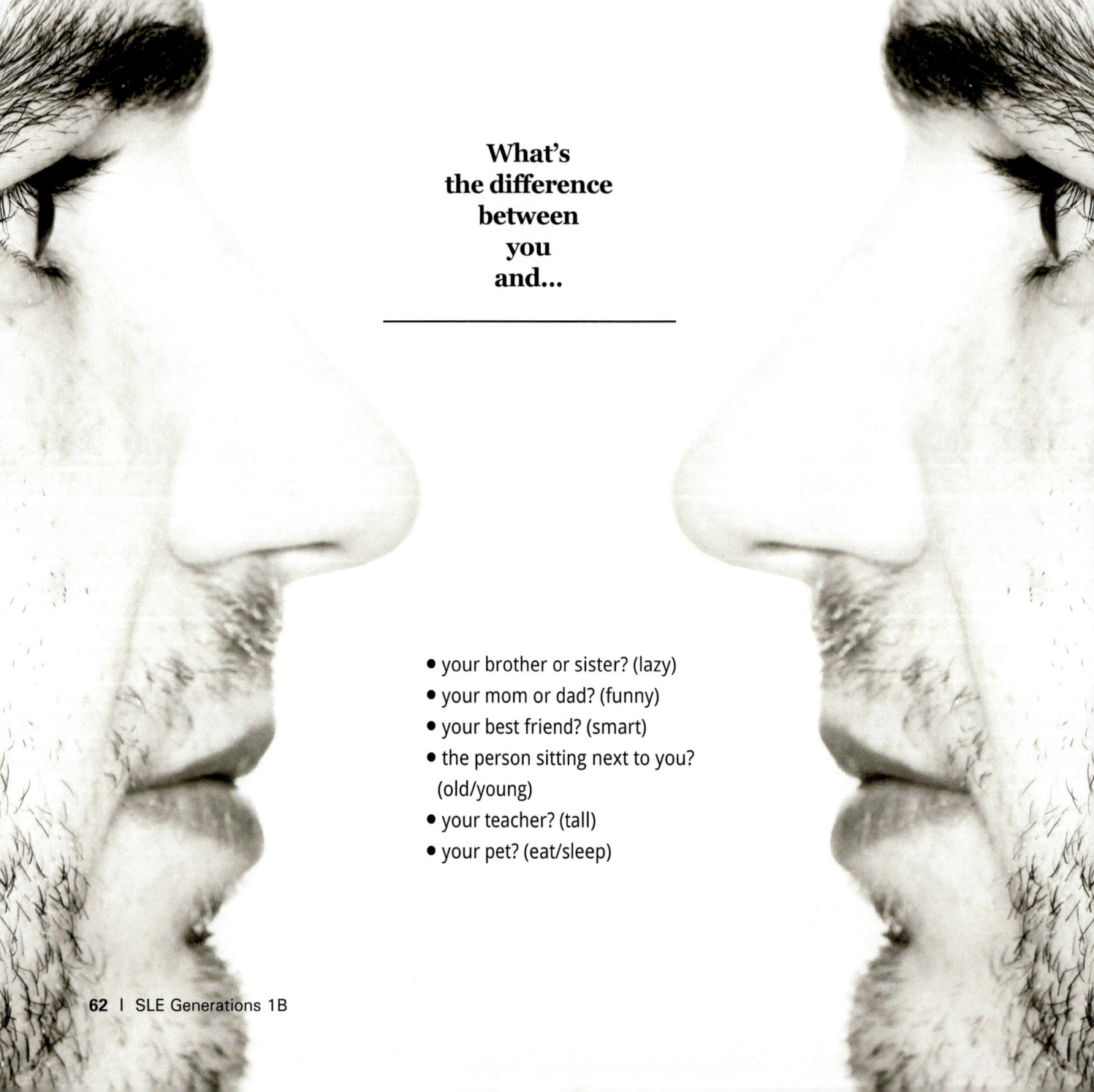

What's the difference between you and...

_____

- your brother or sister? (lazy)
- your mom or dad? (funny)
- your best friend? (smart)
- the person sitting next to you? (old/young)
- your teacher? (tall)
- your pet? (eat/sleep)

A. Far, Far Away

> Where do you live now?
> When did you move there?
> Do you like your neighborhood? Why or why not?

 Café   Supermarket    Golf Course

Park   School   Subway Station

Bowling Alley   Mall   Stadium   Church/Temple

Language Point : Describing Distance

Prepositions are used to describe general distances.

Around- is used in questions about distance.
Is there a café around your house?

Close to + location- says something is not far.
There are several nice cafes close to my house.

Far from + location- says something is not close.
The nearest café is far from my house.

> Look at the map of the local area. Describe which **amenities** are close to or far from where Simon and Mary live.
> Then, ask your partner if there is something similar around his/her house.
> Ask follow-up questions about the place.

Example:
A: *Is there a café close to where Mary lives?*
B: *Yes, it looks like there is one very close to where she lives.*
A: *Are there any cafes around your house?*
B: *Yes, there are many cafes close to me. I like to go to one called Bean Me Up. The coffee is amazing.*

Amenities (*n.*): things around your area that make it a good place to live

B. Moving On Up

Language Point: Describing Differences and Similarities with *as...as*

As...as is used to say that two parts are equal.
The grocery store is **as far as** the café.

Not as...as is used to say the two parts are very different.
The café **isn't as far as** the restaurant.

Tip
The words "nearly" and "almost" are commonly used with "as...as" comparisons.
The café is almost as far as the restaurant.

How can you compare these houses?
Take turns "selling" each house to your partner.

C. This New House

PART 1 • You have been given some land and a **budget** to build the home of your dreams! Your partner is your personal architect, and he or she will help you design your house.
What will you build?

First, choose a general location for your new home:

- ☐ Countryside
- ☐ City
- ☐ **Suburbs**
- ☐ Other

⚠️ You have a total of 16 points to spend on your house. Decide how many points you want to put into each area. You can select the same feature more than once.

```
       Indoor: ____ POINTS

 ☐ Large bathroom       2 pts.
 ☐ Small bathroom       1 pt.
 ☐ Large bedroom        2 pts.
 ☐ Small bedroom        1 pt.
 ☐ Living room          2 pts.
 ☐ Large kitchen        2 pts.
 ☐ Small kitchen        1 pts.
 ☐ Dining room          2 pts.
 ☐ Laundry room         1 pt.
 ☐ Study                2 pts.
 -------------------------------
 Total:                     pts.
```

Budget (*n.*): money for a particular purpose
Suburbs (*n.*): a residential district on the edge of a city

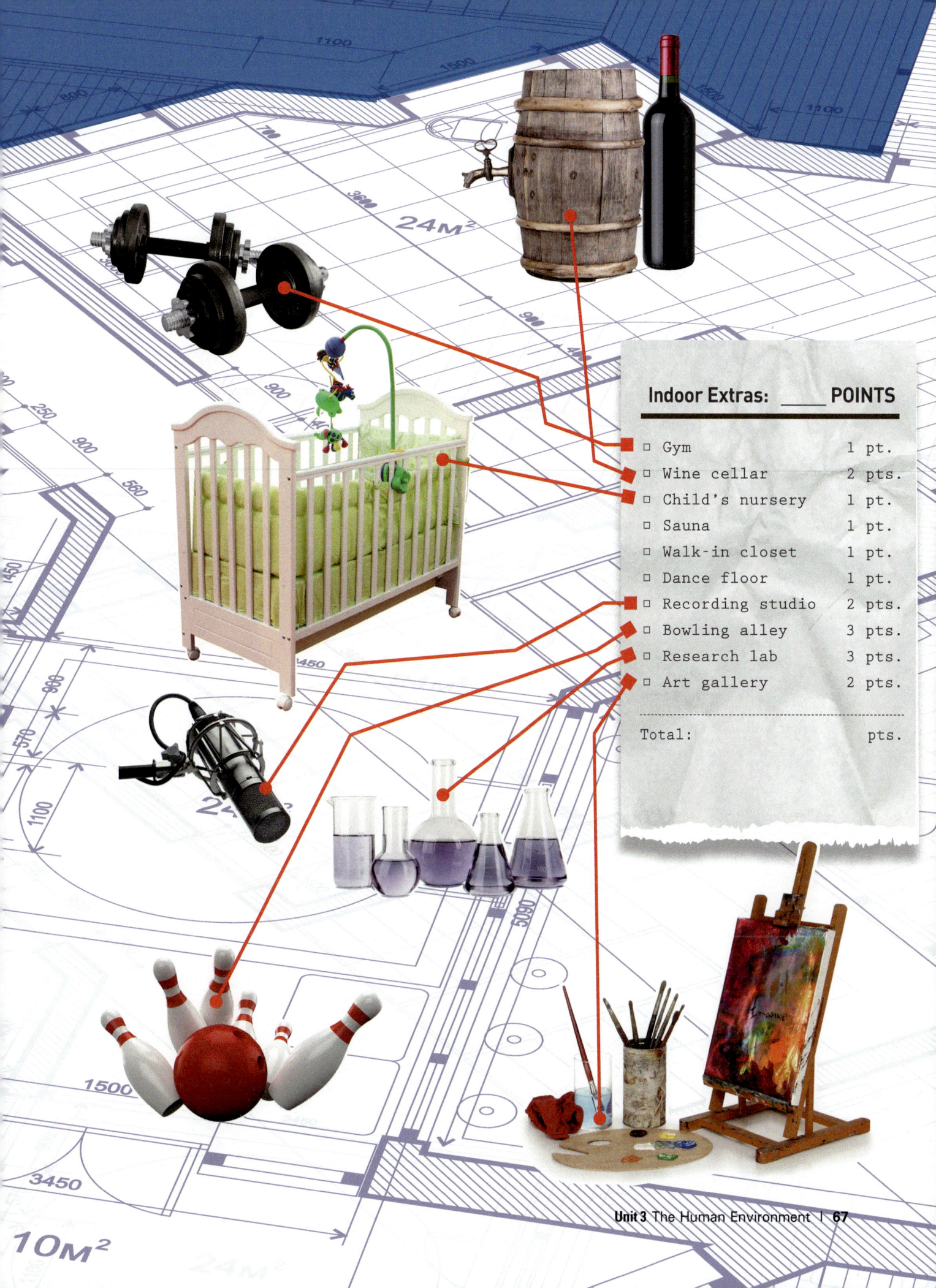

Indoor Extras: _____ POINTS

- Gym — 1 pt.
- Wine cellar — 2 pts.
- Child's nursery — 1 pt.
- Sauna — 1 pt.
- Walk-in closet — 1 pt.
- Dance floor — 1 pt.
- Recording studio — 2 pts.
- Bowling alley — 3 pts.
- Research lab — 3 pts.
- Art gallery — 2 pts.

Total: _____ pts.

Unit 3 The Human Environment | 67

PART 2 • Your house is finished! Discuss what you will do in the following situations.

1 You have a **family reunion** and there are 27 people staying in your house. Where will they stay?

2 Great Aunt Inez died and left you her **poodles**. All twelve of them. What do you do with them?

3 It's 3 a.m. and you wake up to a loud sound of breaking glass. What do you do?

4 You are going on vacation for three weeks. What should you do before you leave?

5 Your boss wants to visit your house. What do you do to make it a very nice visit?

6 You committed a **minor crime** and are under house arrest for six months. What do you do while stuck at home?

7 A musician has moved in next door. He practices his music loudly all day and night, and he's not very good. What do you do?

8 Oh no! You were walking across the street when someone hit you with their car. The woman who hit you gives you a lot of money. You can afford an additional 5 points of upgrades to your house – which will you choose and why?

9 The **economy** is getting bad and all of the local stores and businesses close near your house. What do you do?

10 There is a zombie attack! How can you **survive** without leaving your house?

11 For some reason, you have to sell your house. How much are you going to sell it for? How can you sell the house?

12 At the last minute, you find the money to keep your house. You have a big party to celebrate. What kind of party will you have?

Family reunion (*n.*): a gathering of extended family
Poodle (*n.*): a breed of curly-haired dogs
Minor crime (*n.*): an illegal act that would not lead to jail time
Economy (*n.*): the financial system of a country
Survive (*v.*): to live through difficult conditions

Discussion Questions

1. How many different apartments/houses have you lived in?
   - Can you compare the different places?

2. What is the nicest home you have ever visited?
   - Where was it?
   - Would you like to live there?

3. Which one is better: a nice house in the country or an apartment in the city? Why?

4. Did you ever…? What was it like?
   - Live with your grandparents?
   - Share a room with a brother or sister?
   - Live with a roommate?

5. Which parts of the city do you spend the most time in?
   - Which part of the city is better? Why?

6. Where is the best place you have visited that you never want to live in?
   - Where is the worst place you have visited where you don't want to live?

7. Where is the _____ place to live?
   - safest
   - most dangerous
   - most exciting
   - most boring
   - most modern

UNIT 3 REVIEW

How well can you use…
- ☐ Comparison language?
- ☐ Ways to discuss differences and similarities?

What do you need to study more?

Activity: Apples and Oranges

With a partner, compare the following things.
How are they similar?
How are they different?

Dogs and Cats

> **Example: Motorcycle and Car**
>
> **A:** *How are a motorcycle and a car similar?*
> **B:** *A motorcycle has an engine, and a car has an engine. They both have wheels. How are they different?*
> **A:** *A motorcycle is more dangerous than a car. Cars have more wheels than motorcycles. Cars are bigger.*

Plane

Train

Baseball

Soccer

Your language and English

Laptops

Smart phones

Tomato

Apple

Guitar

Violin

Tea

Coffee

ROOMIES.COM

Segue

Roomies© is the best way to find roommates on the Internet.
We can help you find a place to live or help you find someone to move into your place.

Start | Search | Post a Room | My conversations

From Jones: Hey there, roomie!
I'm looking for someone to help me fill this super cool "artist space". There are no walls, but we could hang curtains to create rooms. It's so big that you can play basketball or ride your bike inside. Cold in the winter, and about a thirty-minute walk to the subway.
$600/month.

From Ahab: Ahoy room-matey!
I have a very small room available for rent on my boat, the S.S. Minnow. There isn't a lot of space, but the view is nice. A twenty-minute walk to the closest bus line.
$400/month.

From Ella: Hello roomies.
I found a great apartment I want to move into in the center of the city. Walking distance to everything! I need two roommates to help me share the cost. There are two bedrooms, so we would have to decide who shares a room.
$300/share or $500/for your own room.

A. Discussion
1. Which one of the above apartments is the best?
   ▶ What makes it better than the others?
2. Which one is the worst?
   ▶ What don't you like about it?

B. Writing
Imagine you live alone in your current apartment or house. Write an advertisement similar to the one above.

04 Frequently Asked Questions

Preferences & Frequency

Objectives:
/ Describe frequency
/ Listen to a dialogue about responsibility

WARM UP

Which of the following things do you do a lot? Which things are most important to you? When was the last time you did this?

- Brush your teeth
- Go to the doctor
- See a movie
- Take a shower
- Buy shoes
- Meet friends
- Eat a sandwich
- Visit the zoo
- Go to class
- Send a message

TONGUE TWISTERS

- A twister of twists often twists a twisted twist twice.

LESSON 1

A. How Often Do You...

Language Point: Describing How Often You Do Things (General)

I	always	breathe (because I have to).
	usually	walk to work (because I work close to home).
	sometimes	eat Italian (because I usually cook at home).
	rarely	take the stairs (because there is an elevator, but sometimes it is broken).
	never	win the lotto (because I don't buy tickets).

Discuss how often you do the following things. Then, answer the question and ask a follow-up question. How often do you...

1. Eat breakfast?

1. What do you eat?
2.

2. Complain?

1. What do you **complain** about?
2.

3. Daydream?

1. What do you **daydream** about?
2.

Complain (*v.*): to say you are unhappy with something
Daydream (*v.*): to have distracting and pleasant thoughts while awake

Frequently Asked Questions

4. Feel scared?
1. What makes you scared?
2.

5. Forget something?
1. What do you forget?
2.

6. Play games?
1. What do you play?
2.

7. See a movie?
1. What kind of movie?
2.

8. Shop for clothes?
1. Where do you shop?
2.

9. Study?
1. What do you study?
2.

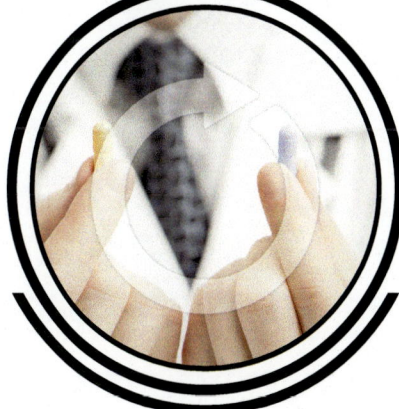

10. Get sick?
1. Do you worry about **germs**?
2.

Germs (*n.*): viruses or bacteria

B. Adventures in House Sitting

Language Point: Describing How Often You Do Things (Specific)

Another way to answer a "how often" question is by giving a specific amount.

Once		a minute.
Twice		an hour.

Three		a day.
Four	times	a week.
Five		a month.
Six		a year.

Every other (hour, day, week, etc.)

You can also ask for a specific amount: How many times + time + yes/no question.
How many times a year do you go to the doctor?

Pre-listening

Ask one of the questions from **the Warm Up** a second time.
This time ask your partner to be more specific.

Example: How often do you brush your teeth?
A: *I always brush my teeth!*
B: *How many times a day?*
A: *Three or four times a day.*

Listening TRACK 8-9

Nick is going to be taking care of the house while his parents go on a second honeymoon. Check how often Nick should do each thing in the boxes.

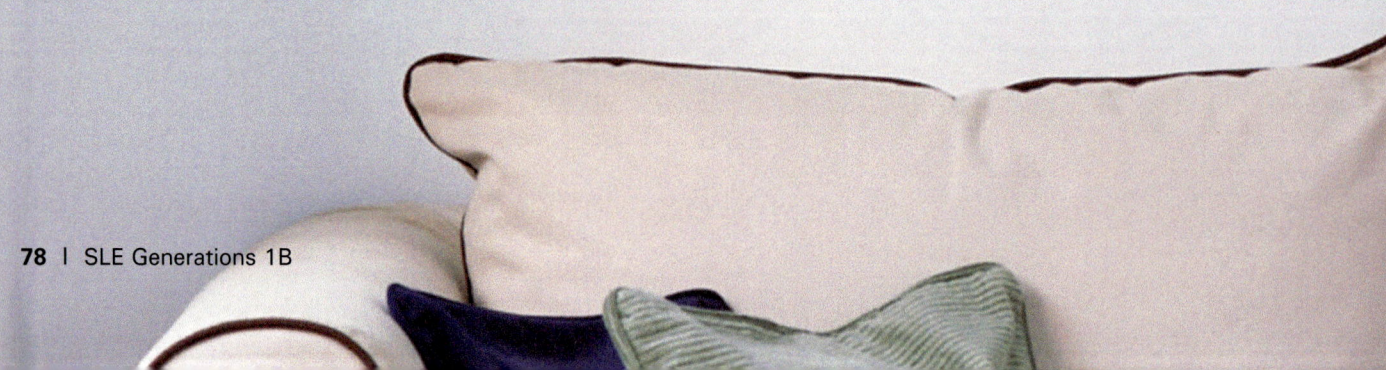

78 | SLE Generations 1B

1. Woofy the dog

Feed:
once ☐
twice ☐
a day

Walk:
always ☐
usually ☐
after dinner

2. Chewy the cat

Feed:
once ☐
three times ☐
a day

Change box:
every ☐
every other ☐
day

3. Bobby the brother

Eat vegetables:
rarely ☐
once a day ☐

Take medicine:
always ☐
never ☐
after every meal

4. The plants

Water:
once ☐
four times ☐
a week

Play music:
sometimes ☐
all the time ☐

Unit 4 Frequently Asked Questions | 79

Post-listening

Ask your partner for some advice about important things you should or shouldn't do.

How often should I…?
You should…

Hang out with grandma

Clean the house

Change my socks

> **Example**:
> How often should I feed the fish?
> **A:** *You should feed it frequently.*
> **B:** *You should feed it at least once or twice a day.*

Study English

Get a haircut

Watch TV

Take a vacation with friends

Take a taxi

Drink coffee

How often should I....
You should...

Get married

Get my resume photo taken

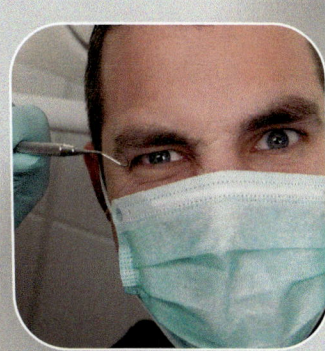
Go to the dentist

Unit 4 Preferences & Frequency | 81

C. I'm a Pepper

1 Choose who goes first in your group. Then, pick a topic to ask a question about.

- [ ] Food
- [ ] Family
- [ ] Shopping
- [ ] School
- [ ] Work
- [ ] Sports/Hobbies
- [ ] Travel
- [ ] Friends
- [ ] Technology

Example:
I choose food.

2 Think of a question to ask your group in that category. It can be a "how often" question, but it doesn't have to be.

Example:
What is something you never eat?

3 Everyone answers by saying two things that are true and one thing that is a lie.

Example:
*I never eat peppers.
I never eat pizza.
I never eat ice cream.*

4 The person who asked the question must then guess which one each person is lying about.

Example:
*You're lying about the pizza.
Everyone eats pizza.*

5 Each person should give an explanation for their lie.

Example:
Actually, I can't stand pizza, but I am crazy about spicy peppers!

Discussion **Questions**

1. Do you ever get headaches?
   - How long do they usually last?

2. How much sleep do you get?
   - Do you think it's enough or not enough?

3. Do you ever **skip** breakfast?
   - Do you ever skip dinner?
   - Why?

4. How often do you eat…
   - at home?
   - out with your family?
   - out on a date?

5. How often do you go to the salon?
   - How much time do you usually spend there?

6. How much time do you spend exercising each week?
   - What kind of exercise do you like?

7. Where do you most frequently take trips to?
   - What do you do while you are there?

Skip (v.): to not do something you usually do

LESSON 2

>> WARM UP

Objectives:
/ Give reasons for preference
/ Make decisions

What kind of ... do you like? Why?

I ♥
- Sports
- Food
- Cars
- Music
- Movies
- Clothes

A. Decisions, Decisions

Language Point: Asking About and Giving Reasons for Preference

	Informal	Formal
Asking about preference	*Do you like A or B?*	*Which one do you prefer, A or B?*
Expressing preference	*B's better because…*	*I prefer A to B because…*

With your partner(s), take turns answering the following questions. Be sure to give reasons for your preferences.

Do you like _____ or _____?

- taking a taxi/taking the bus
- eating Western food/eating Chinese food
- eating with a knife and fork/eating with chopsticks
- studying English/studying another language
- to live in a big city/to live in the country
- to relax at home/to exercise
- to take the subway/to take the bus
- to watch a drama/to watch the news

Which one do you prefer, _____ or _____?

- having a big family/having a small family
- watching movies at home/watching movies at a theater
- going to a night club/going to a bar
- climbing a mountain/lying on a beach
- spring/fall
- coffee/tea
- classical music/rock music
- pants/shorts

B. Living Life Dangerously: A Quiz

● Do you think you are an adventurous person, or do you prefer to **play it safe**? Why do you think so?

Some people like to take **risks**. Others like to live a very safe life. What kind of person are you? Take the following quiz and find out. For each pair of options, choose one. Then take turns explaining your choices to your partner(s).

Which is better... Do you prefer...

A

- ☐ 1. New kinds of food
- ☐ 2. Driving fast
- ☐ 3. The twentieth floor
- ☐ 4. Traveling alone
- ☐ 5. Motorcycles
- ☐ 6. Scuba diving in the ocean
- ☐ 7. Bungee jumping
- ☐ 8. Drinking heavily
- ☐ 9. Spending money
- ☐ 10. A dangerous job

safe or dangerous?

Play it safe (*exp.*): be careful
Risk (*n.*): a chance of something going wrong

☐ 1. Food you are familiar with
☐ 2. Driving the speed limit
☐ 3. The first floor
☐ 4. Traveling with a group
☐ 5. Bicycles
☐ 6. Swimming in a pool
☐ 7. Watching someone bungee jumping
☐ 8. Drinking a little
☐ 9. Saving money
☐ 10. A safe but boring job

Did you have more A or B answers?

Result Box

More than 50% A	A = B	More than 50% B
You enjoy taking risks and trying new things. You live life on the wild side!	You live a very well-balanced life. You know how to have fun, but you make wise decisions!	You are a very safe and responsible person! You will have a long, comfortable life!

Do you agree with your result?

C. Build an Amusement Park

PART 1 ● Make a choice based on you and your partner(s) preferences. For each category, explain why your choice is better than the other choices.

What is the theme of your amusement park? Why do you choose _____ ?
- General
- Space
- Wild West
- Fantasy
- Other

1 What kind of food will you have at the park? Choose one. Why that kind of food?
- Cheap n' Greasy
- Organic Veggie Delight
- Ice Cream and Sweets

2 What quality of souvenirs will you sell? Choose one. What are some examples of things people can buy?
- High Quality, Expensive
- Low Quality, Cheap

3 What special shows will you have? Choose one. How often will the shows be held?
- Laser Shows
- Parades
- Fireworks

4 How will people get around at your park? Choose two.
- Children's railway
- Monorail
- Animals
- Moving walkway

5 You can hire some extra staff – who will you choose? Choose one. Why is that group important?
- More Characters
- More Security

PART 2

Now that you've built your amusement park, discuss what you will do in the following situations.

1. You rarely get many older people visiting your park.
2. Kids are always **throwing up** after they ride the Extreme Rollercoaster.
3. The park has bad weather every other month. How could you bring more customers during rainy months?
4. There are sometimes problems with **pickpockets** at the park!
5. Congratulations – your park received an award for being the Best New Amusement Park. You can add one new attraction. Which one will you choose?

Throw up (*phrasal v.*): to empty the contents of the stomach through the mouth
Pickpocket (*n.*): a thief who steals from people's pockets

Discussion Questions

1. Which brands do you think make good quality products?
   - Why do you prefer them to other brands?

2. What are the names of the different…in your city?
   - telecom companies
   - movie theaters
   - coffee chains
   - shopping areas
   - Which one do you prefer in each category?

3. Why do you think some people prefer to do dangerous things and others prefer to play it safe?

4. Who chose the last place you went to on vacation?
   - Did that person make a good choice?

5. What kind of job do you prefer:
   - Sitting or standing?
   - Outside or inside?
   - Talking or writing?

6. Do you think it's easy to choose or do you have a hard time?
   - Do you know anyone who is very good at choosing?
   - How about someone who is very bad?

7. Do you think there are too many choices in life or not enough?

UNIT 4 REVIEW

How well can you use…
- ☐ Expressions for describing frequency?
- ☐ Ways to give preference?

What do you need to study more?

Activity: White Elephant

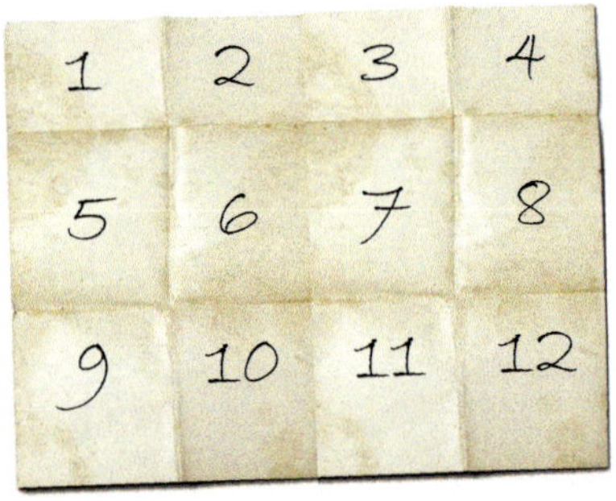

Make numbered slips of paper, cut the slips up, and put them face down on the table. (Alternate: Copy the pictures, cut them up, and put them face down on the table.)

Rules:

- Decide who goes first.
- The first person takes a card. The number on the card corresponds to the "gift" he/she receives. The first person can choose to keep this gift, or pass it to the next player and draw a new card.
- The second player can choose to keep the gift that was passed to him/her. OR pass the gift to the next player and draw a card. OR steal the first player's gift.
- If your gift is stolen, draw a card.
- The game ends when it goes around the circle once. The first player has the option at the very end to steal the gift of the last person to play.

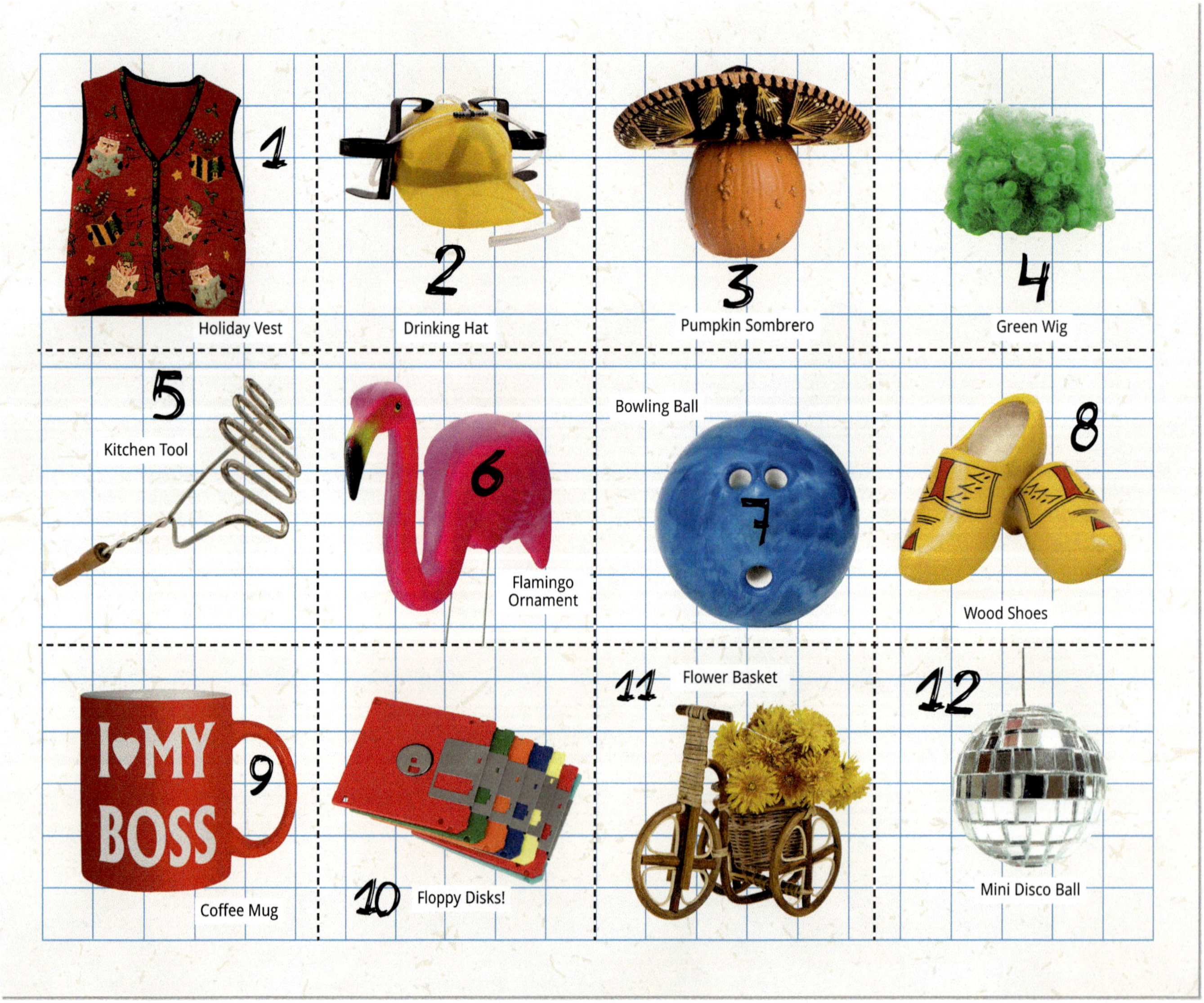

1. Holiday Vest	2. Drinking Hat	3. Pumpkin Sombrero	4. Green Wig
5. Kitchen Tool	6. Flamingo Ornament	7. Bowling Ball	8. Wood Shoes
9. Coffee Mug	10. Floppy Disks!	11. Flower Basket	12. Mini Disco Ball

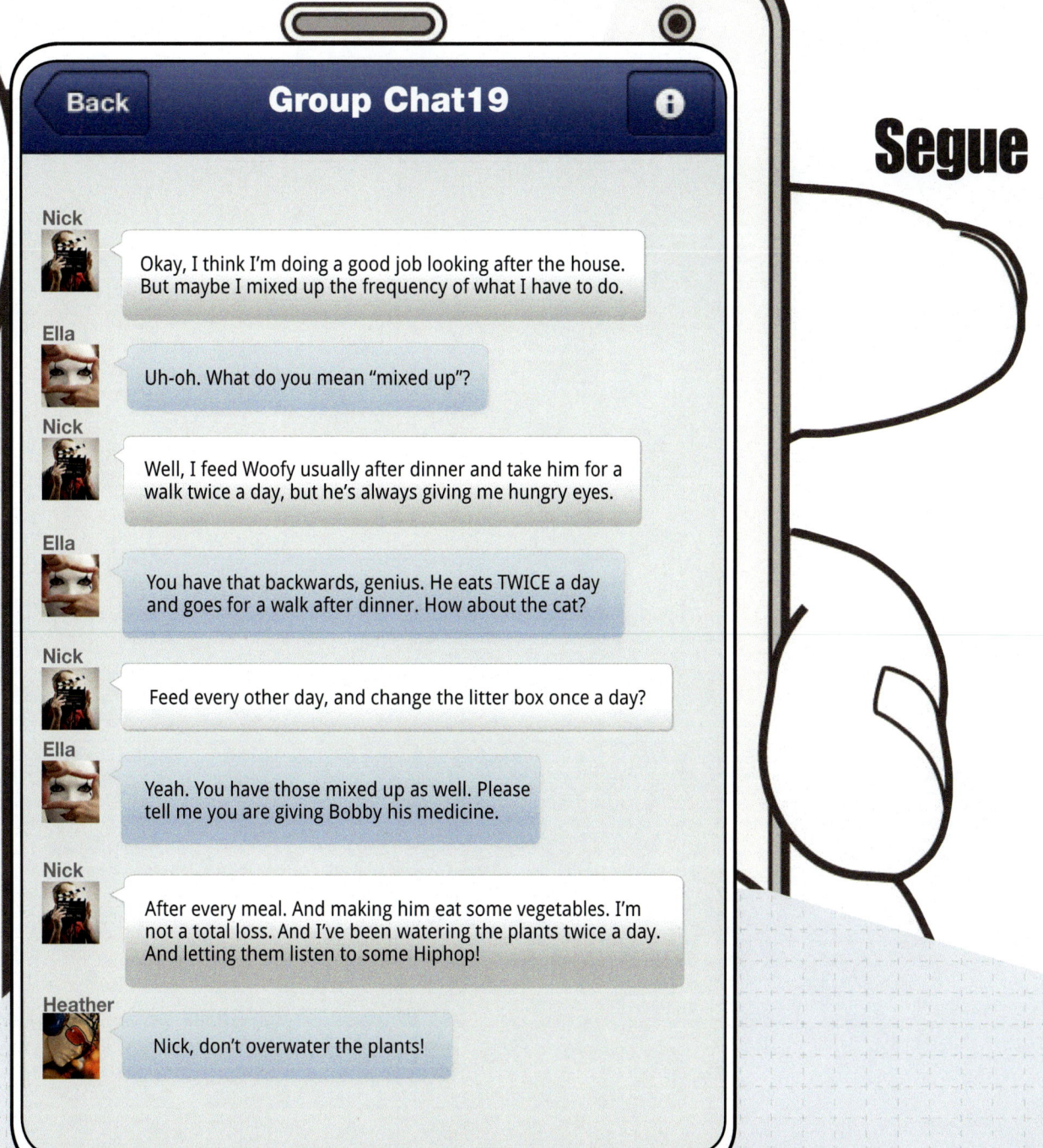

Segue

A. Discussion
1. Do you have anything you have to take care of? (A pet, plants, family member, etc.)
   ▶ What do you have to do to take care of it?
2. What things do you own that require service?
   ▶ Do you ever get them serviced?

B. Writing
Imagine you are going on a long vacation and you need to have a friend take care of your house. Write him/her a short list of things they have to do. Think about:

▶ Pets
▶ Plants
▶ Mail
▶ Cleaning
▶ Trash

Unit 4 Frequently Asked Questions | 93

05
Where Were You When
Moments in Time

Objectives:
/ Describe when events happened
/ Listen to someone describe events in the past

WARM UP

Answer the following questions, and compare your answers with your partner's.

What time did you wake up this morning?
You: _____   Your Partner: _____
• Who woke up earlier?

What was the first thing you did?
You: _____   Your Partner: _____
• Which was more interesting?

How did you get here?
You: _____   Your Partner: _____
• Which one was quicker?

What time did you eat dinner yesterday?
You: _____   Your Partner: _____
• Who ate earlier?

What did you eat?
You: _____   Your Partner: _____
• Which was more delicious?

TONGUE TWISTERS

• When the doctor doctored the doctor, did the doctor doing the doctoring doctor as he wanted to be doctored?

LESSON 1

A. When I Was Your Age

Language Point : Describing "When" Things Happened

When is used for an event that happens immediately after another event, or at nearly the same time.

When I opened the front door, my cat ran outside!

While is used for events that happen at the same time.

Gillian cleaned the glass while Tyrion did the dishes.

Tip:
When and *While* can be very confusing. Native speakers will often use *When* for either situation.

Ron continued to play the violin when/while the bear attacked him.

Match any statement from column A to a statement in column B using *When* or *While*. Then explain what happened or why it happened. Change the pronoun (I/he/she/they) if necessary.

> **Example: Jane opened the door**...
>
> *when her friends yelled "Surprise!"*
> *...because it was her birthday, and she was very happy.*

	A	B
1	Jane opened the door.	She/he caught a giant fish.
2	Irene was seven years old.	He/she had a picnic.
3	Mandy was taking a shower.	The police **knocked** on the door.
4	Ken was eating breakfast.	He/she met the Jones family.
5	Charlie was fishing by the river.	He/she started **choking**.
6	The Smith family was traveling in Europe.	She/he found the perfect dress.

	A	B
1	Becky was shopping at the mall.	The **power went out**.
2	Clyde was flying to Vancouver.	He/she fought a bear.
3	Lenny was studying in the library.	Her/his friends yelled, "Surprise!"
4	Warren went to the gym.	Rob and Roy were **robbing** his/her house.
5	Sylvia was at the park.	He/she started to feel sick.
6	Mary was watching television with Fred.	He/she realized he was **out of shape**.

Knock (*v.*): to hit a door to gain attention
Choke (*v.*): to stop breathing because of a blocked throat
Power went out (*idiom*): lost electricity
Rob (*v.*): to take something illegally from a person using force
Out of shape (*idiom*): in poor physical condition

B. Where Were You?

Language Point : Past Progressive and Simple Past

The past progressive is used to express an action that was ongoing in the past.
Ella was sleeping.

When + the *simple past* is used with the past progressive to show that something stopped the action.
Ella was sleeping when the phone rang. ("The phone rang" is in the simple past.)

While + *past progressive* when used with the simple past has the same meaning.
While Ella was sleeping, the phone rang.

Pre-listening

Ask your partner what he/she was doing last week. After he/she tells you, compare it to what you were doing at the same time.

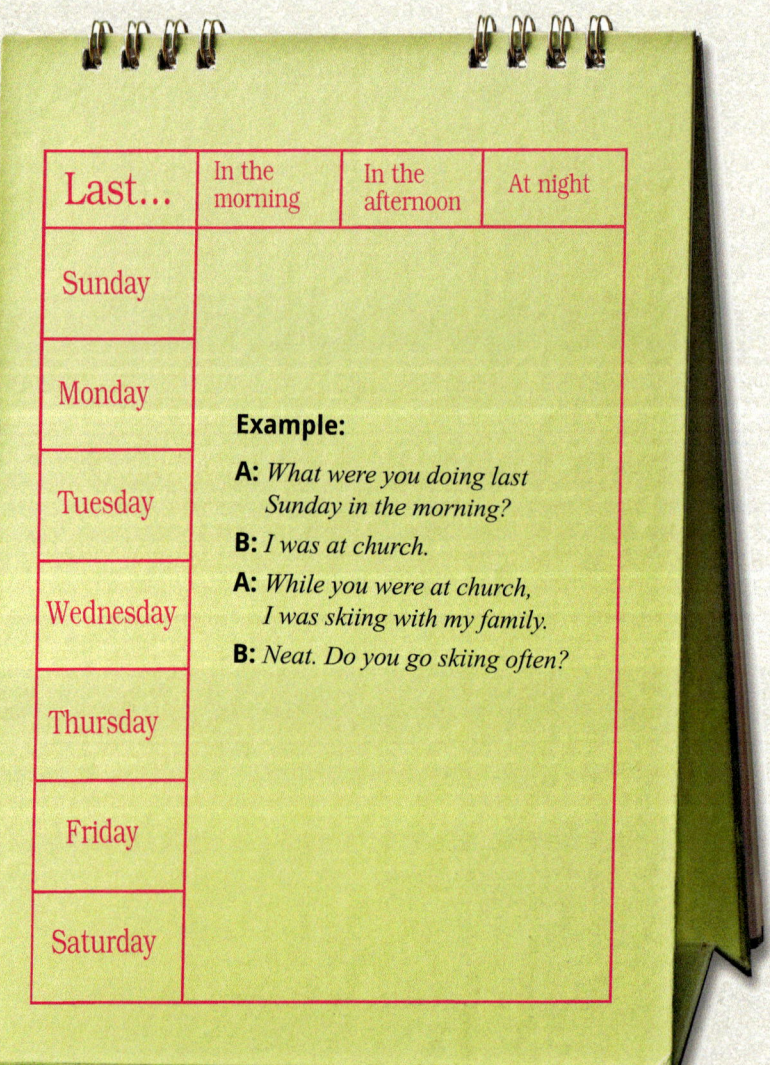

Last...	In the morning	In the afternoon	At night
Sunday			
Monday			
Tuesday			
Wednesday			
Thursday			
Friday			
Saturday			

Example:

A: *What were you doing last Sunday in the morning?*
B: *I was at church.*
A: *While you were at church, I was skiing with my family.*
B: *Neat. Do you go skiing often?*

Listening TRACK 10-11

Bobby wants to go to the library and called his sister many times to get a ride. Look at the pictures and guess what Ella was doing at each time. Then, listen to her on the phone with Bobby and circle the activity that she **said** she was doing.

When Bobby called, Ella was…

Post-listening

1 Ella was lying about her day!
What was Ella really doing at each time?

2 What were you doing yesterday while Ella was…?

C. Multitasking

PART 1 • Look at the situations below. Is it okay to do these things at the same time? Why or why not? If not, when is it okay?

Example: Sleeping while studying in the library.
It's not okay! I think it's rude to sleep in the library because…

PART 2 • Make up your own statements about doing things at the same time.
Is it okay to _____ while _____?

Example:
A: *Is it okay to **dance** while **talking**?*
B: *I guess so, but people might look at you funny.*

Sample word bank:

Sleep	Talk
Drive	Study
Eat	Dance
Cry	Laugh
Work	Yawn
Talk on the phone	Yell
Watch a ____	
Ride (the bus/the subway/in a taxi)	
Fight	
Swim	

100 | SLE Generations 1B

Discussion Questions

1. What were you doing before class began?
   - ▶ Who were you with?

2. Where were you living ten years ago?
   - ▶ Who were you living with?

3. What were you buying the last time you bought something?
   - ▶ Where were you shopping?

4. What were you watching the last time you watched TV?
   - ▶ Do you watch that show often?

5. What were you eating the last time you ate?
   - ▶ Where were you eating?

6. Where were you going the last time you took a taxi?
   - ▶ From where to where?

7. Where were you flying the last time you flew?
   - ▶ From where to where?

LESSON 2

>> WARM UP

Objectives:
/ Ask for more information about past stories
/ Compare the past of others to your own

Guess what your partner or teacher was doing yesterday at the following times:

Yesterday at _____ I think you were _____.

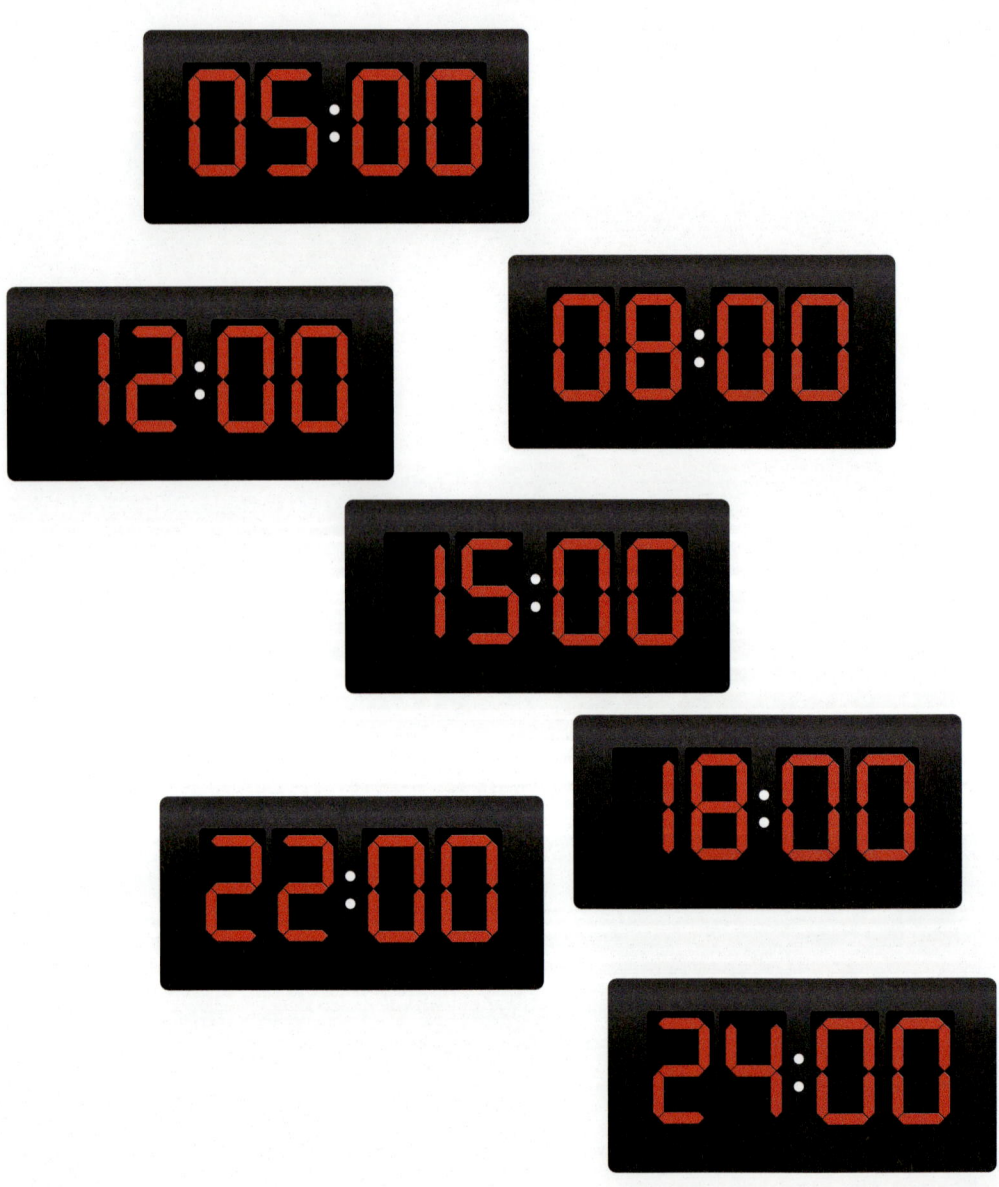

A. What Happened Here?

Language Point : Asking About What Happened Next

- When telling a story it's common to describe something in the past progressive.
- The action is stopped when something happens.
- You can ask, "What happened next?" to get more information.

Example:

A: *Jeb was climbing a ladder when he slipped and fell.*
B: *What happened next?*
A: *His friend called an ambulance!*

PART 1 • Finish the sentence with something that stops the action. Ask your partner, "What happened next?", and continue the story.

1. Mcfly was buzzing around when...

2. Gerald was running for the phone when...

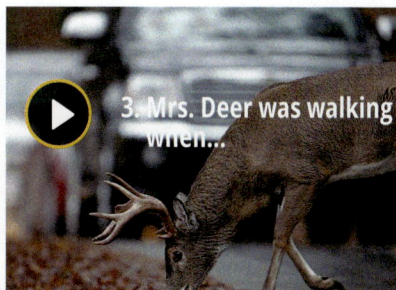
3. Mrs. Deer was walking when...

4. Peter was sending a text when...

5. Missy was taking a test when...

6. Dean was grilling some burgers when...

7. Jake was standing next to a cliff when...

8. Carter was writing a paper when...

Unit 5 Where Were You When | 103

B. You Think You Had a Bad Day?

You will control a day in Bill's life. What kind of day will you give him? Will you be kind and give him the best day ever, or will you make sure he has a terrible day? For each situation, choose what happened and ask a follow-up question.

> **Example: When Bill woke up...**
>
> ...he had a healthy breakfast. He ate a grapefruit and a piece of toast.

1. **When Bill woke up...**
   a. ...he had a healthy breakfast. What did he eat?
   b. ...he realized he was late for work. Why did he wake up late?

2. **While he was getting ready for work...**
   a. ...he found money in his pants.
   b. ...he couldn't find his keys.

3. **On his way to work...**
   a. ...he was stuck in traffic.
   b. ...he got a seat on the subway.
   c. ...he spilled coffee on his shirt.

4. **When he got to work...**
   a. ...his boss yelled at him.
   b. ...his co-worker brought him coffee.
   c. ...someone spilled coffee on him.

5. **At lunch...**
   a. ...his server brought him the wrong meal.
   b. ...his boss paid.

8 In the evening...
a. ...he had a relaxing night with his cat.
b. ...he had an exciting date with his girlfriend.
c. ...his kitchen caught fire when he tried to cook.

7 On his way home...
a. ...he was stuck in traffic.
b. ...he got a seat on the subway.
c. ...he spilled coffee on his shirt.

9 When he went to bed...
a. ...he had a peaceful sleep.
b. ...the neighbors had a loud party.
c. ...he spilled coffee on his shirt.

6 In the afternoon...
a. ...he fell asleep at his desk.
b. ...he had a long, boring meeting.
c. ...he was given the afternoon off.
d. ...he was fired.

What do you think was the best and worst part of his day?

C. Our Story

When Jim and Kim were born, they were accidently separated.

> Look at the things Jim and Kim were doing at different ages of their lives.
> Which person made a better decision at each age in your opinion?
> What were you doing at that age? OR What do you think you will be doing at that age?

Jim	Age	Kim
1. Jim studied hard in school.	15	Kim was interested in dating and his **social life**.
2. Jim went to university.	18	Kim traveled for a year.
3. Jim was studying hard.	20	Kim met the woman of his dreams.
4. Jim got his first job.	22	Kim had his first child.
5. Jim got married.	25	Kim started an internship.
6. Jim got a big **promotion**.	28	Kim started his own company.
7. Jim had his first child.	35	Kim took a year off to travel.
8. Jim became president of the company.	44	Kim had his second kid.
9. Jim **retired**.	55	Kim continued to work.
10. Jim traveled the world.	60	Kim retired.

Jim met someone who looks exactly like him in a park.

62

It was Kim! The brothers were finally reunited!

Social life (*idiom*): the time available for friends and family
Promotion (*n.*): advancement in position
Retire (*v.*): to end working permanently

Discussion Questions

1. What were you talking about the last time you talked on the phone?
   ▶ What happened next?

2. What happened the last time you were in a fight or an **argument**?
   ▶ What happened next?

3. What were you doing the last time you hurt yourself?
   ▶ What happened next?

4. When was the last time you were lost?
   ▶ What were you doing?

5. Where were you the last time you were with a lot of people drinking?
   ▶ What happened next?

6. When was the last time you lost something?
   ▶ Did you ever find it?

7. What happened the last time you had a big test?
   ▶ What was the result?

UNIT 5 REVIEW

How well can you use…
- ☐ Ways to describe when events happened?
- ☐ How to ask about what happened next?

What do you need to study more?

Argument (*n.*): a fight had with words

Activity: You're Getting Warmer

- Write an answer in each of the boxes. If you can't remember exactly when you did it, just make a guess.
- Hide what you wrote from your partner.
- Next, ask your partner the questions. Your partner should guess when you did it.
- Tell your partner if he/she is getting closer by using the expressions:

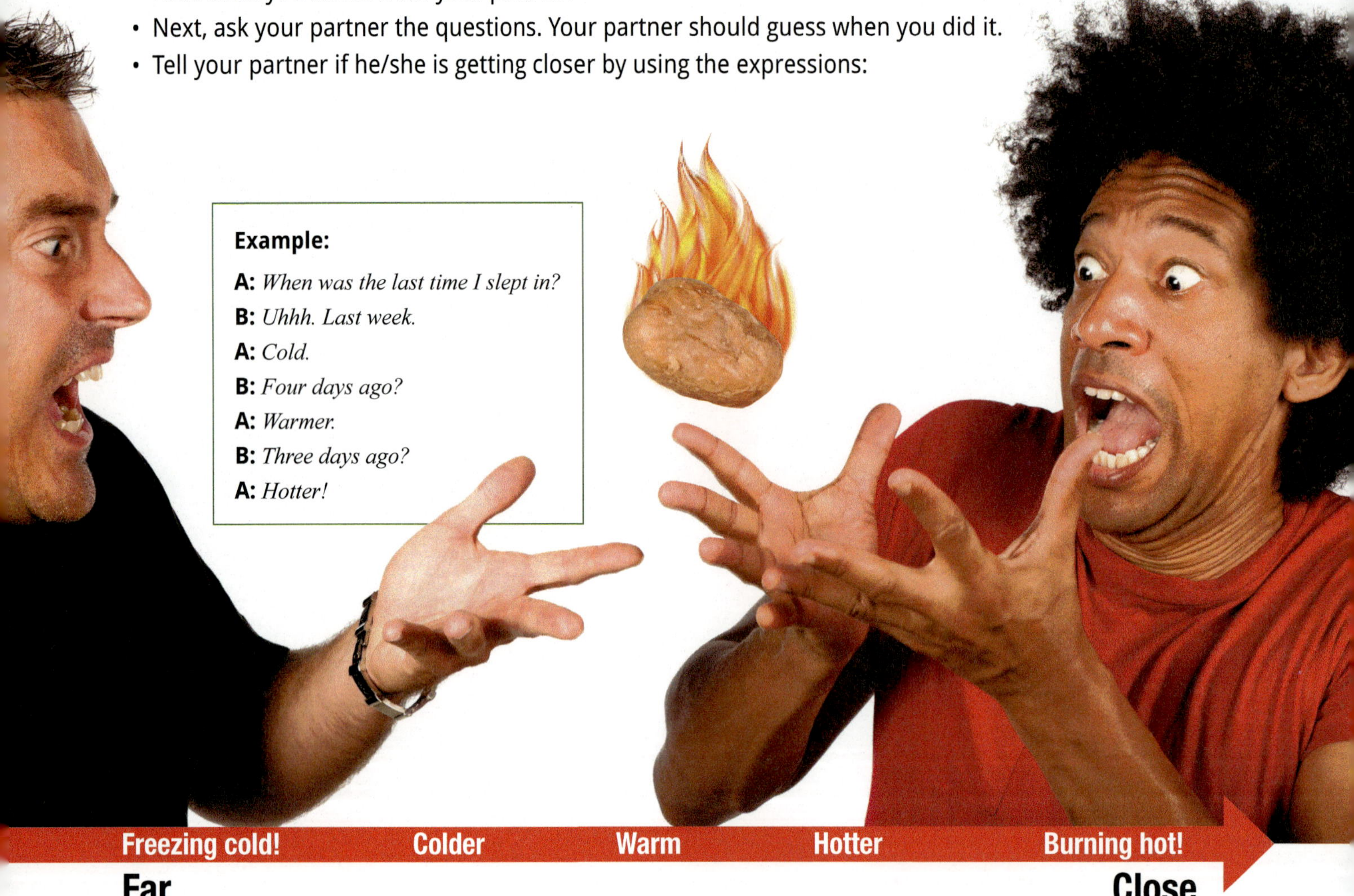

Example:
A: *When was the last time I slept in?*
B: *Uhhh. Last week.*
A: *Cold.*
B: *Four days ago?*
A: *Warmer.*
B: *Three days ago?*
A: *Hotter!*

Freezing cold!   **Colder**   **Warm**   **Hotter**   **Burning hot!**
Far   **Close**

When was the last time I...

Slept in?	Went to the dentist?	Took a taxi?	Played video games?	Got my hair cut?
Ex. *(Yesterday)*				
Wrote a letter?	Went on a blind date?	Went hiking in the mountains?	Drank tea?	Argued with my parents?
Got up before 6 a.m.?	Went out dancing?	Visited my relatives?	Stayed up late studying?	Traveled outside the city?
Went shopping?	Wore shorts?	Saw a movie?	Lost money?	Was late to work?

Ella:
Such a good day! Slept in until lunch time. Met some friends. Went shopping. Ate delicious food. I want more days like this!

 **Tammy:** I saw you sleeping at the library around 4:30!

 Ella: Haha, yeah. I have a test next week, but I needed a nap after all that food.

 Bobby: Wait a second, sis. You told me you were doing work all day!

 Nick: Busted.

 Ella: What can I say? Being me is hard work!

 Bobby: ...

A. Discussion
1. Is it more acceptable to lie to a family member than it is to lie to a friend or coworker?
2. Have you ever made up an excuse for why you couldn't do something? What happened?

B. Writing
Write down your schedule for tomorrow and compare it with a partner.

06
Mixed Feelings
Feelings & Friends

Objectives:
/ Describe feelings
/ Listen to two people discuss how animals feel

WARM UP

Look at the picture of the rainbow below. What is a good and bad emotion you can think of for each color?

Angry
Sad
Happy
Excited
Scared
Lonely
Shy
Jealous
Etc.

Unit 6 Mixed Feelings | 111

LESSON 1

A. All In a Feeling

Language Point : Asking About and Describing Feelings

When do you feel…?
Do you ever feel…?
What makes you feel…?
How often do you feel…?

Adjectives that describe feelings:
Positive: Ecstatic / Happy / Proud / Hopeful / Calm / **Content**
Negative: Indifferent / Nervous / Jealous / Sad / Hurt / Terrible / Angry / Afraid

PART 1 ● Ask your partner how he/she thinks the person feels. Then, ask a follow-up question about when or what makes your partner feel like that.

Example:
A: *How do you think this person feels?*
B: *I think she is happy because she has a big smile.*
A: *What makes you feel happy?*

How do you think this person feels? Why?

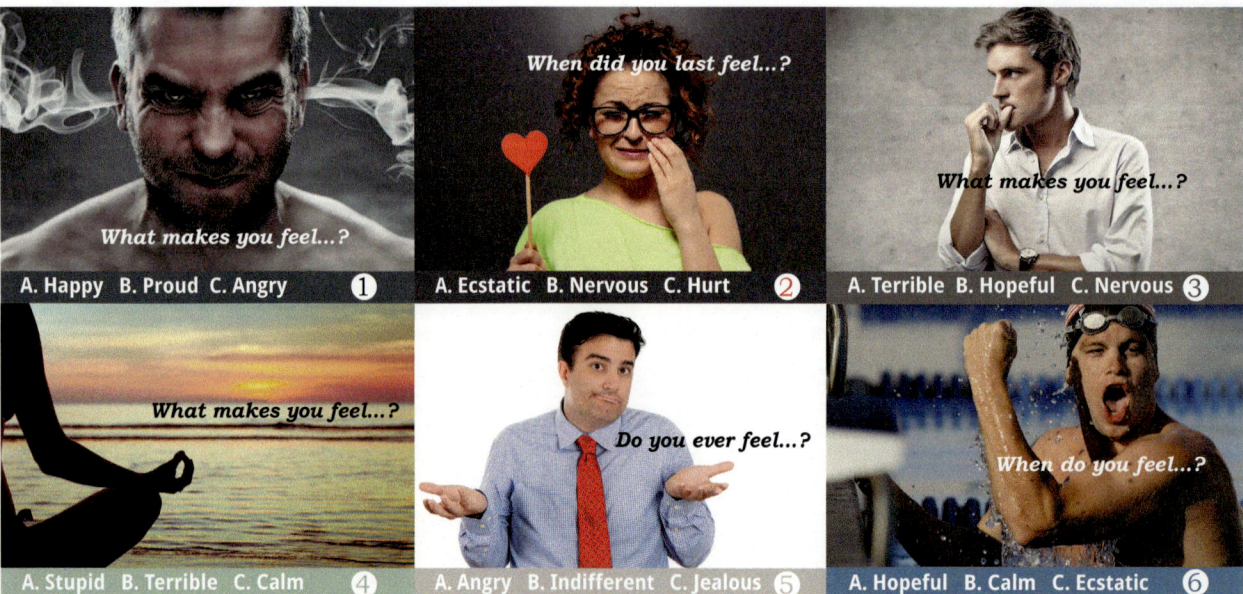

1. A. Happy B. Proud C. Angry
2. A. Ecstatic B. Nervous C. Hurt
3. A. Terrible B. Hopeful C. Nervous
4. A. Stupid B. Terrible C. Calm
5. A. Angry B. Indifferent C. Jealous
6. A. Hopeful B. Calm C. Ecstatic

Language Point : Verbs Used as Adjectives

Adding *–ed* to certain verbs is used to describe how a person feels. In this case, the verbs are just like adjectives.

Positive: Thrilled / Interested / Excited / Relieved / Surprised
Negative: Bored / Worried / Embarrassed / Annoyed / **Depressed**

PART 2 • Discuss with your partner how the following things make you feel. Ask your partner to give a reason why he/she feels that way.

How do you feel about...

Example:
A: *How do you feel about waiting in line?*
B: *I'm usually annoyed.*
A: *Why do you feel annoyed?*
B: *The people ahead of me take so long and ask a lot of questions!*

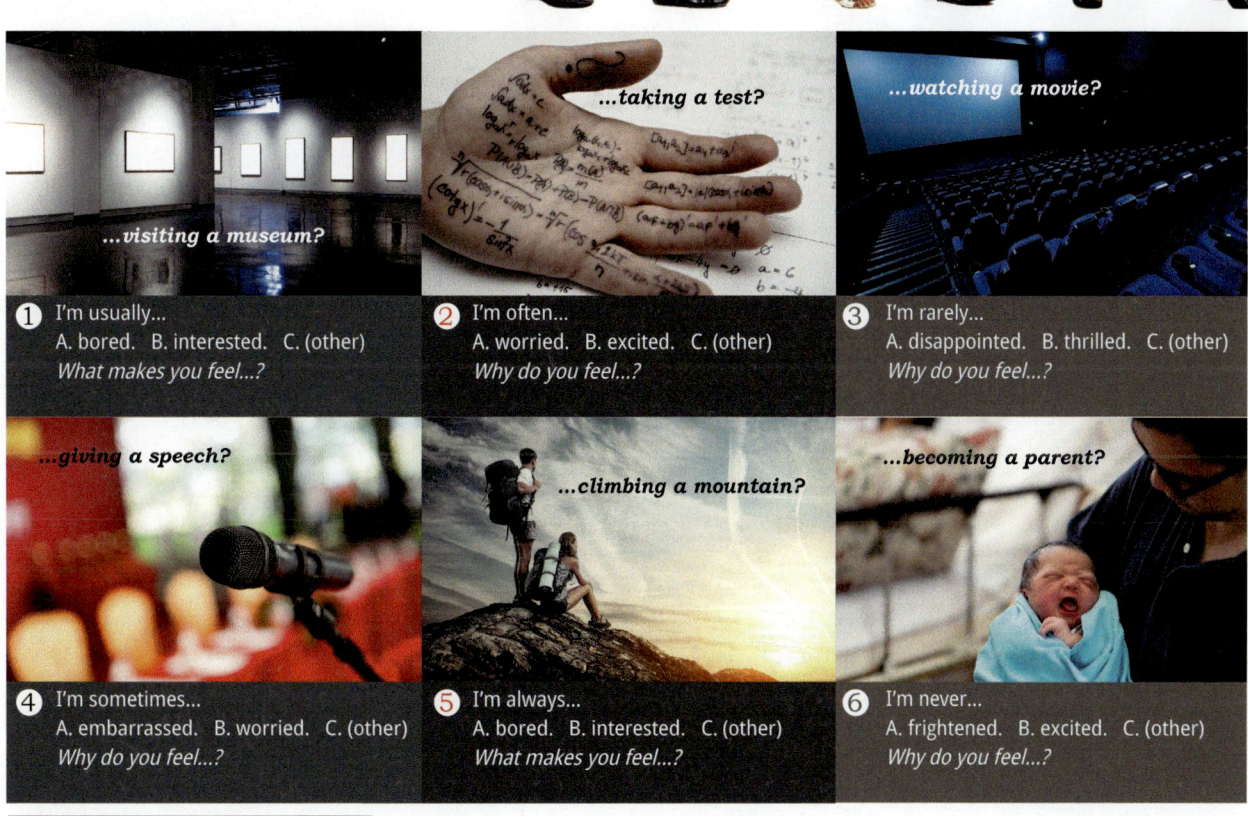

① ...visiting a museum?
I'm usually...
A. bored. B. interested. C. (other)
What makes you feel...?

② ...taking a test?
I'm often...
A. worried. B. excited. C. (other)
Why do you feel...?

③ ...watching a movie?
I'm rarely...
A. disappointed. B. thrilled. C. (other)
Why do you feel...?

④ ...giving a speech?
I'm sometimes...
A. embarrassed. B. worried. C. (other)
Why do you feel...?

⑤ ...climbing a mountain?
I'm always...
A. bored. B. interested. C. (other)
What makes you feel...?

⑥ ...becoming a parent?
I'm never...
A. frightened. B. excited. C. (other)
Why do you feel...?

Ecstatic (*adj.*): extremely happy
Content (*adj.*): quietly satisfied
Indifferent (*adj.*): without care or interest
Thrilled (*adj.*): very excited
Depressed (*adj.*): very unhappy or hopeless

B. Scaredy Cat

Pre-listening

1. Do you think animals have feelings? Why or why not?
2. Look at the pictures below.
   - How do you think the animals feel?
   - Why do you think they feel that way?

Possible Adjectives:

Sad / Excited / Proud / Bored / Tired / Happy / Lonely / Nervous / Worried

Elephant

Snails

Example: Mantis

A: *How do you think the mantis feels?*
B: *She looks pretty ecstatic.*
A: *Why do you think she's ecstatic?*
B: *She probably just ate a good meal.*

Pig

Orangutan

Owl

Listening TRACK 12-13

Listen and circle the way Heather thinks the dog and cat feel.

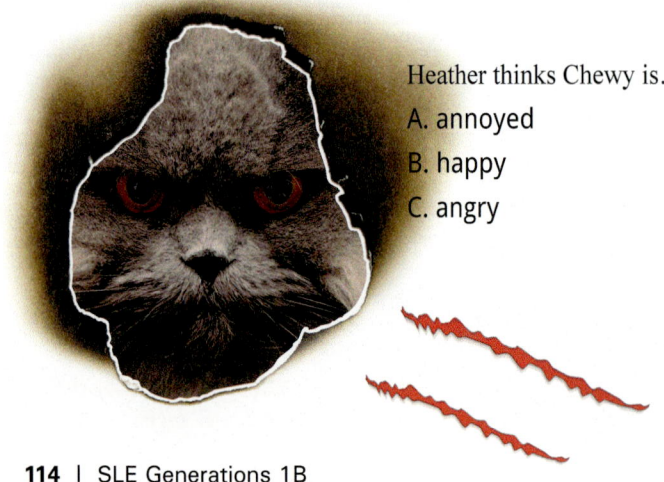

Heather thinks Chewy is…
A. annoyed
B. happy
C. angry

Heather thinks Woofy is…
A. sad
B. nervous
C. content

Post-listening

Choose a feeling from the box. Ask your partner, "Why were you _____ at the _____?"
Give your partner a reason why you would feel that way at that place.

> **Example:**
>
> **A:** *Why were you excited at a **funeral**?*
> **B:** *I was excited because I saw a celebrity.*
> **A:** *That's terrible.*
> **B:** *I know. Don't hate me.*

Possible Adjectives:

Ecstatic / Proud / Calm / Content / Nervous / Jealous / Sad / Angry / Afraid / Excited / Confused / Bored / Worried / Embarrassed

2. On a date

3. At a water park

4. At an airport

5. At a diner

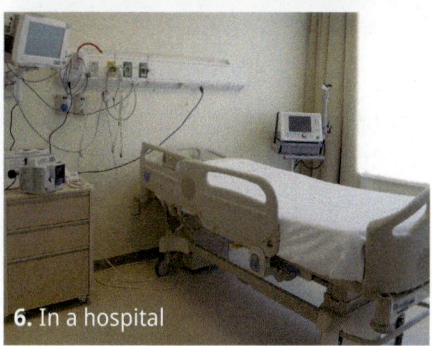
6. In a hospital

1. At a funeral

Funeral (*n.*): ceremony for someone who died

C. Emotional Rollercoaster

> Circle one letter for each sentence.
> Then, insert the word related to each letter to make a story.
> Share your story with your group.
> Each person in the group should take a turn telling the story, and answer the follow-up questions.

Story 1
1 I was (A) (B) (C)
2 to (A) (B) (C)
3 when a (A) (B) (C)
4 (A) (B) (C) me!
5 It was (A) (B) (C)!
6 (A) (B) (C)

1 a. walking	b. running	c. **crawling**
2 a. school	b. work	c. my house
3 a. bear	b. baby	c. clown
4 a. hugged	b. attacked	c. fed
5 a. wonderful	b. terrifying	c. interesting

Read it like you are: 6 a. happy   b. sad   c. confused

Follow up:
1 Why were you (#6)?
2 Why were you going to (#2)?
3 What are you going to do next?

Story 2
1 I am so (A) (B) (C)!
2 I just (A) (B) (C)
3 my (A) (B) (C)…
4 but I have to meet my (A) (B) (C)
5 at the (A) (B) (C) in a few hours.

1 a. angry	b. ecstatic	c. nervous
2 a. ate	b. lost	c. **broke**
3 a. phone	b. leg	c. bicycle
4 a. doctor	b. friend	c. **ex**
5 a. beach	b. grocery store	c. airport

Follow up:
1 Why were you (#1)?
2 Why are you meeting your (#4) at the (#5)?
3 What will you do about your problem?

Crawl (*v.*): to move on hands and knees
Broke (*v.*): damaged
Ex (*n.*): former girlfriend/boyfriend or spouse

Discussion **Questions**

1. Are you an emotional person?
   - ▶ Do you usually express your feelings or hide them?

2. What feelings do you enjoy having?
   - ▶ Which ones do you hate having?

3. How often do you express your positive or negative feelings in the following ways?
   - ▶ Crying
   - ▶ Laughing
   - ▶ **Cursing**
   - ▶ Touching
   - ▶ Yelling or shouting

4. When do animals feel…
   - ▶ happy?
   - ▶ sad?
   - ▶ excited?
   - ▶ scared?
   - ▶ jealous?

5. Do you have a pet? Did you ever have a pet?
   - ▶ Which emotions does/did it show?

6. When in your life have you felt these emotions very strongly?
   - ▶ Happy

LESSON 2

>> WARM UP

Objectives:
/ Describe possibility
/ Discuss friendships

> Choose an emotion from the box and make a gesture that represents it.
> Your partner will guess which emotion you're representing.

Ecstatic/ Proud / Calm/ Content / Nervous / Jealous / Sad / Angry / Afraid / Excited / Confused / Bored / Worried / Embarrassed

Example:
A: *I think you are unhappy. What are you unhappy about?*

A. Anything's Possible

Language Point: Using Would To Ask Yes/No Questions

Would is used in questions to stress possibility.

Yes/No Questions:

Would + You / He / She / It / We / They + Verb + Question?

A: *Would you eat snails?*   *Would she be happy singing with friends?*   *Would they like to go to a movie?*
B: *Yes, I would. I'd try anything.*   *Yes, she would. She loves singing.*   *No, they wouldn't. They're busy.*

Ask your partner "yes/no questions" using *would*. Give a reason why you would or wouldn't like doing the following activities.

Tip: *Would you* is often pronounced as one word in casual conversation.

Example:

Woodja come and get me around 8 o'clock?

Would you be happy...?

1 spending a night out drinking and dancing with friends?

Example:

A: *Would you be happy spending a night out drinking and dancing with friends?*
B: *No, I wouldn't. I don't drink and I can't dance.*

2 ordering a pizza and staying at home?

3 jumping out of an airplane?

4 lying on the beach all day?

5 exercising in the gym?

6 going to an amusement park?

7 shopping for three hours?

8 taking a class?

B. Which One of Your Friends

superlatives

Language Point : Using *Would* To Ask Information Questions

Information Questions:

| Where / Who / What / When / Why / How | would | you / he / she / we / they | verb |

Example:

A: *Where would you go?*
B: *I'd go to a Chinese restaurant.*

A: *Who would you take with you?*
B: *I'd take my girlfriend.*

A: *What would you eat?*
B: *I'd eat noodles.*

Which one of your friends...

1 ...is the most handsome/beautiful?
 • Would he/she win a beauty contest?

2 ...lives the farthest from you?
 • Where would you like him/her to live?

3 ...is the tallest?
 • Would you like to be taller than him/her?

4 ...is the most athletic?
 • Who would win in a foot race? You or him/her?

5 ...is the most talkative?
 • Would he/she make a good MC?

6 ...have you known the longest?
 • When would you like to see him/her next?

7 ...has the most brothers and sisters?
 • Would you like to have the same number of brothers and sisters?

8 ...is the richest?
 • What would you like to have that he/she has?

9 ...is the smartest?
 • How would your friend do in this class?

10 ...is the funniest?
 • Would you like to be as funny as your friend?

C. How to Make (or Lose) a Friend in Seven Weeks

PART 1 • You're about to make a new friend (or enemy). Choose one of these three people to make into a new friend (or enemy) to last a lifetime. Each week, decide what to do with your friend and give specific examples. Explain your choices!

Friend #1: Eddie Dean
Who he is: Police officer; likes painting; likes saving money; former child actor

Friend #2: Susannah Holmes
Who she is: Intern at dentist office; loves to sing; hates cleaning; very independent

Friend #3: Tabby Callahan
Who she is: Retired school teacher; loves her dog; hates crowded places

Week 1 — You've just met your new friend! Where would you take your friend to eat dinner?

Choice A — McBurger Town
- Eddie: ♥♥♥
- Susannah: ♥
- Tabby: ♥♥

Choice B — Fancy-sounding French restaurant
- Eddie: ♥
- Susannah: ♥♥♥
- Tabby: ♥

Choice C — MegaBuffet
- Eddie: ♥♥
- Susannah: ♥♥
- Tabby: ♥♥♥

Choice A
Megamall clothes shopping
- **Eddie:** ♥
- **Susannah:** ♥♥♥
- **Tabby:** ♥♥♥

Choice B
Local street market
- **Eddie:** ♥♥
- **Susannah:** ♥
- **Tabby:** ♥♥

Week 2
Your new friend wants to do some shopping. Where would you go?

Choice C
Online shopping
- **Eddie:** ♥♥♥
- **Susannah:** ♥
- **Tabby:** ♥

Choice A
Camping/hiking
- **Eddie:** ♥♥♥
- **Susannah:** ♥♥
- **Tabby:** ♥

Week 3
You and your friend decide to do something exciting. What exciting thing would you do?

Choice C
Movie marathon
- **Eddie:** ♥
- **Susannah:** ♥♥♥
- **Tabby:** ♥♥

Choice B
Amusement Park
- **Eddie:** ♥♥
- **Susannah:** ♥
- **Tabby:** ♥♥♥

GO!

Unit 6 Mixed Feelings | 123

Week 4

Your friend wants you to set them up on a blind date. You know a...

Choice A

Nerdy quiet type

Eddie: ♥♥
Susannah: ♥♥
Tabby: ♥

Choice B

Corporate climber

Eddie: ♥
Susannah: ♥♥♥
Tabby: ♥♥

Choice C

Athletic party animal

Eddie: ♥♥♥
Susannah: ♥
Tabby: ♥♥♥

Week 5

You and your friend get in a fight. Why do you think you got in the fight? What would you do after the fight?

Choice A

Send an apology text.

Eddie: ♥♥♥
Susannah: ♥
Tabby: ♥♥♥

Choice B

Buy a gift.

Eddie: ♥
Susannah: ♥♥♥
Tabby: ♥

Choice C

Wait for him/her to apologize.

Eddie: ♥♥
Susannah: ♥♥
Tabby: ♥♥

Nerdy (*adj.*): very interested in technical or scientific subjects
Corporate climber (*idiom*): someone interested in becoming successful at a company

Week 6

Your friend had something terrible happen to them and needs some support. How would you help?

Choice A
Leave him/her alone. He/she needs some time.

Eddie: ♥♥
Susannah: ♥
Tabby: ♥♥

Choice B
Take him/her out for a few drinks.

Eddie: ♥♥♥
Susannah: ♥♥
Tabby: ♥

Choice C
Take him/her out for a weekend getaway to forget their problems.

Eddie: ♥
Susannah: ♥♥♥
Tabby: ♥♥

Week 7

Your friend's birthday is coming up! How would you celebrate?

Choice A
Outdoor BBQ party

Eddie: ♥♥♥
Susannah: ♥♥
Tabby: ♥♥

Choice B
Jazz club that serves excellent wine and cheese

Eddie: ♥
Susannah: ♥♥♥
Tabby: ♥♥

Choice C
Two words: Milkshake Party!

Eddie: ♥♥
Susannah: ♥
Tabby: ♥

Unit 6 Mixed Feelings | 125

PART 2

Add up the number of hearts you've earned from week 1 through week 6.
Depending on the number of hearts you've earned, you'll find out if you've got a real friend or a real enemy!

Eddie's Score Table

♥	Description
7	Watch your back. He is planning to destroy your life.
8-10	He's saying bad things about you to others, and he doesn't answer your calls.
11-13	He becomes one of those MyFaceWorld friends you never actually talk to, but sometimes 'like' his status updates.
14-17	You guys still **hang out** now and again, but usually only with a group of other people.
18-20	You've become pretty good friends and hang out every other weekend.
21	You've made a friend for life! He paints you on his wall!

Susannah's Score Table

♥	Description
7	You run into her at the mall with other friends. She pretends to not know who you are.
8-10	She keeps saying that you two should hang out more, but then is always "busy" when you ask her to go do something.
11-13	She thinks you are a reliable friend and not very clingy.
14-17	She hangs a picture of you on her wall! Best friends for life!
18-20	She hangs a picture of you on her wall, and uses it to play darts.
21	She runs away every time she sees you. She even changed her phone number.

Tabby's Score Table

♥	Description
7	Tabby considers you one of her closest friends. You're like family now!
8-10	She invites you to play cards at least once a week.
11-13	You two meet for coffee occasionally, but she sometimes brings her new best friend.
14-17	She only calls you when she needs someone to walk her dog.
18-20	She doesn't answer your calls and you're not getting a Christmas card this year.
21	She REALLY doesn't like you. You think she is the one leaving dog poop in front of your door.

hang out (*v.*): to spend time together

Discussion Questions

1. What would make you feel very _____
   - Relaxed?
   - Stressed?
   - Happy?
   - Unhappy?

2. Would you ever…
   - …steal food to feed your family?
   - …go skydiving?
   - …move to another country?

3. Which of your friends would…
   - …make a good husband/wife?
   - …be a good actor/actress?
   - …be a good president?

4. How would you spend $100,000,000 you won playing a lottery?

5. How well do you know your best friend? Tell your partner:
   - how you met
   - his/her personality
   - his/her physical features
   - what kind of things you do together

6. Do you have an enemy?
   - Why is this person your enemy?

7. Do you have any friends you don't see anymore?
   - Would you like to see him/her now?
   - What do you think he/she is doing these days?

UNIT 6 REVIEW

How well can you use…
- ☐ Different ways to describe feelings?
- ☐ Ways to describe possibility?

What do you need to study more?

Activity: Face Your Feelings

Look at the faces below and describe either what makes you feel that way, or the last time you felt that way.

presents.com

World Politics Justice Entertainment Tech Health Living Travel Opinion iReport Money Sports

PNN presents

This Week in Animal Advice:

Segue

Expert Animal Advice with Dr. Kitty Feelgood

SquigglesFan247 asks:

Hi, Dr. Kitty! I have a problem with my cat. At night, he plays and runs around the house a lot. He wakes me up at least three times every night. When I don't get much sleep, I feel terrible in the morning. I don't know what to do. It is making me very sad. I love him, but I am very annoyed at his late night activities!

Dear SquigglesFan247,

I am not surprised to hear this problem. It is a very common problem for many cat owners. Cats are naturally night animals, so they are more awake when you want to sleep! There are a few options you can try. He may feel bored at night. Try playing with him in the evening. Also, cats get tired after a big meal. Feed him right before you go to bed. Finally, look around the house or outside. Maybe there is something making him feel nervous or frightened. A dog next door? A bird in the attic?

Try these things and maybe you will not feel so tired in the morning.

Sincerely,

Dr. Kitty Feelgood

A. Discussion
1. Do you agree with this advice? Why?
2. What are some other common problems people have with pets?

B. Writing
Write a pet problem and exchange it with a partner. Write an advice column to help solve that problem.

WARM UP

What things do you need:

1 To make a cup of tea?

2 To travel to the North Pole?

3 To lift a large rock?

4 To build a house?

5 To go camping?

TONGUE TWISTERS

- Two witches are watching two watches, so which witch is used to watch which watch?

LESSON 1

A. Riddle Me This

Example: Anchor
What is something you drop when you need it but pick up when you don't?
• Clue: You use it to keep the boat from moving.

> Choose Student A or Student B.
> You will ask your partner the riddles below.
> Your partner can ask you for a clue if he/she needs one.

Riddles

STUDENT A
Ask Student B these riddles:

1 What teaches but cannot talk?
• Clue: You use it for studying.

2 What is full of holes but can hold water?
• Clue: You use it to wash the dishes.

3 What has two hands but no arms and legs?
• Clue: You use it for telling time.

4 What kind of room has no doors and windows?
• Clue: You use it to make soup.

5 What cannot be used until you break it?
• Clue: You use it to make an omelet.

6 What has many keys but cannot open doors?
• Clue: You use it to make music.

7 What has teeth but cannot bite?
• Clue: You use it for cutting wood.

STUDENT A

• These are the answers to the riddles Student B is asking.
• If you have trouble finding the answer, ask Student B for a clue.

 Table  Gloves  Carrot  Comb  Needle  Towel  Umbrella

> Choose Student A or Student B.
> You will ask your partner the riddles below.
> Your partner can ask you for a clue if he/she needs one.

Riddles

STUDENT B
Ask Student A these riddles:

Example: Anchor
What is something you drop when you need it but pick up when you don't?
• Clue: You use it to keep the boat from moving.

1 What gets wet while drying?
• Clue: You use it for drying after a shower.

2 What has four legs but no feet?
• Clue: You use it to eat with the family.

3 What goes up when the rain comes down?
• Clue: You use it to keep dry.

4 What has fingers and thumbs but no arms?
• Clue: You use them for keeping warm.

5 What is orange and sounds like a parrot?
• Clue: You use it to make a delicious stew.

6 What has teeth but no mouth?
• Clue: You use it for **straightening** your hair.

7 What always has to work with something in its eye?
• Clue: You use it to sew a button on.

STUDENT B

• These are the answers to the riddles Student A is asking.
• If you have trouble finding the answer, ask Student A for a clue.

Piano

Mushroom

Sponge

Saw

Egg

Book

Clock

Straighten (v.): to make something into a straight line

B. Lifehack

Language Point : Describing Purpose With *Used To* and *Used For*

To ask about purpose the preposition *for* is used:
*What is this thing used **for**?*

To describe a purpose both *to* and *for* are used:
For is followed by a gerund (-ing)
This is used for...
This is used for cutting pizza.

To is more common in speaking:
This is used to...
This is used to cut pizza.

Pre-listening

Ask your partner the questions on the left. Answer your partner with the purposes on the right.

What is _____ used for?

1. a paper clip 
2. nail polish 
3. a dustpan 
4. dental floss 
5. a clothespin

It is used to/for _____.

A. clean your teeth
B. connecting pieces of paper
C. hanging clothes to dry
D. color your nails
E. cleaning up trash

What are _____ used for?

1. pasta noodles
2. cupcake wrappers
3. straws
4. sticky notes
5. hair pins

They are used to/for _____.

A. baking cupcakes
B. make spaghetti
C. writing messages
D. drinking beverages
E. keep hair out of your eyes

Listening TRACK 14-15

Grandpa Henry is good at thinking of new uses for common items. Listen to the conversation and circle the way Grandpa says he uses the item.

Sponge:
- A. Cleaning the dishes
- B. As an ice pack
- C. Painting a picture

Walnut:
- A. Ice cream topping
- B. Fixing scratches in furniture
- C. As ear plugs

Unit 7 Give Me a Hint | 135

Post-listening

Look at the pictures with a partner. How are the items from the pre-listening used in these pictures? Do you know of any other life hacks?

Cupcake wrapper

> **Example: Cupcake Wrapper**
> **A:** *What is the cupcake wrapper used for?*
> **B:** *It's used to catch the drips from the popsicle. That's pretty good.*

- Lighting a candle
- Hold a nail
- Cutting a cake
- Fill a bucket with water
- Holding cords
- Taking the stem out of a strawberry
- Keeping the toothpaste at the front of the tube
- Cover thread so the button doesn't come off
- Get dirt out of the keyboard

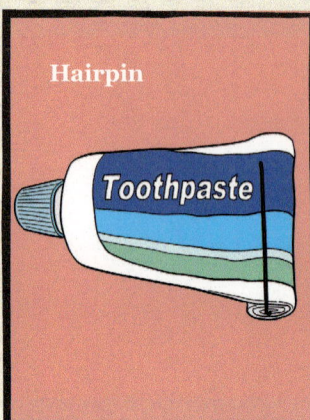

Hairpin

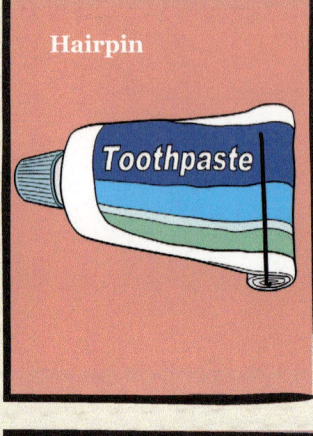

Straw

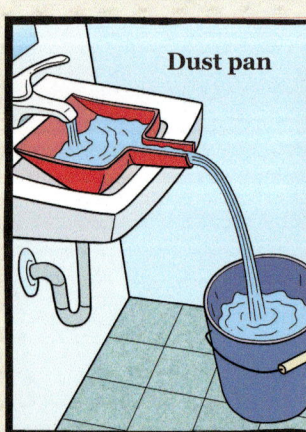

Dust pan

Sticky note

Fingernail polish

Paper clip

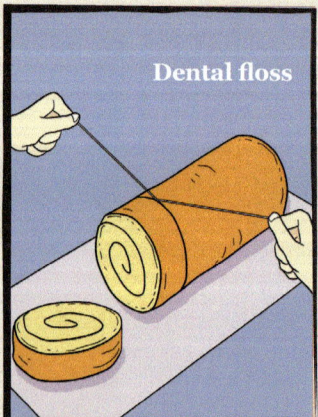

Dental floss

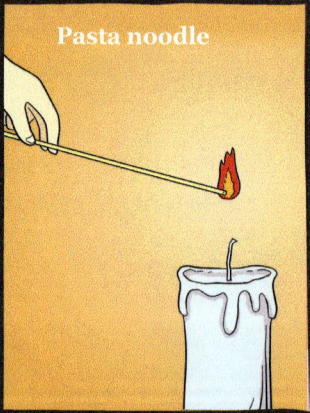

Pasta noodle

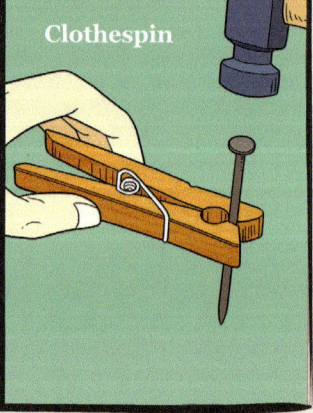

Clothespin

C. Survivor

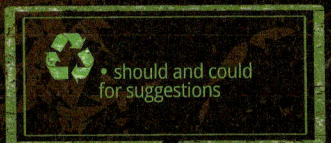

You and your partners were flying when the plane crashed! You are all okay, but you don't know where you are. You must walk out of the mountains, but you can only take five items. How will you survive?

PART 1 • Choose the five items you will need to survive.
Discuss what you can use each item for, and give a reason why it's important.

We could use the _____ for _____.
We should use the _____ to _____.

○ BOTTLED WATER

○ TOILET PAPER

○ ROPE

○ MATCHES

○ MIRROR

○ SIX-PACK OF BEER

○ SNOW SKIS

○ SLEEPING BAG

○ COMPASS

○ PORTABLE GAS STOVE

○ MAGAZINES

○ KNIFE

○ PISTOL

○ 3 CANS OF FOOD

○ MAP

PART 2 •

Finding your way home. Discuss what you can do in the following situations.
While you are walking out of the mountains...

1 ...you get hungry.

> **Example:**
> *We should eat the cans of food.*

2 ...you meet a bear.
3 ...you get bored at night.
4 ...there is a terrible snow storm.
5 ...you get chased by angry bees.
6 ...you find some mushrooms.
7 ...a plane flies by.
8 ...it gets really cold.
9 ...you find a hidden cave.
10 ...you come to a big deep river.

Discussion Questions

1. Do you like solving puzzles?
   - Do you know any riddles?

2. Can video games be educational?
   - Do you think games can be used to teach people? Why or why not?

3. What do you think is the most useful invention? Why?
   - What do you think is the worst invention? Why?

4. What is a problem you always have?
   - What invention could solve your problem?

5. Are these necessary or **luxury** items?
   - Computer
   - Smart phone
   - Car
   - Cosmetics
   - Coffee
   - Alcohol

6. What are three things that you always want to have with you?
   - What do you usually use these items for?

7. Take something out from your pocket, wallet, or bag.
   - What do you use it for?
   - Where did you get it?
   - Why did you get it?

Luxury *(adj.):* desirable but not essential

LESSON 2

>> WARM UP

Objectives:
/ Express necessity
/ Make choices and give advice

Imagine that you could take a magic pill to change something, but you can only choose one.
Which one would you choose, and why?

Use the blue pill to:
make yourself younger

Use the red pill for:
speaking perfect English

Use the white pill to:
make yourself smarter

Use the green pill for:
making yourself luckier

Use the purple pill to:
make yourself stronger

Use the yellow pill for:
(Other)

A. A Necessary Evil

Language Point: Expressing Necessity

UNNECESSARY	NECESSARY
Don't have to	**Have to**
- Expresses that something is not necessary or is unimportant.	- Expresses that something is necessary or really important.
The boss said we don't have to come to the meeting.	*The boss said everyone has to come to the meeting.*

Tip: Have got to
Have got to is often used in informal speaking. It has the same meaning as *have to*, and is usually contracted. *I've got to go. I promised my friend I would meet him.*

PART 1 • Discuss the **necessities** in life. Make questions using the different times in the boxes below.

1 What is something you have to do _____?

today   to stay alive
tomorrow   when going overseas
next week   while driving a car
soon   when visiting relatives

• What don't you have to do _____?

2 What is something you had to do _____?

yesterday   last week   last year
when you were in high school
when you were in elementary school
while you were in the army
when you started working/university

• What didn't you have to do _____?

Necessities (*n.*): something that is essential for life

Unit 7 Give Me a Hint | 141

Language Point: *Should* vs. *Have to*

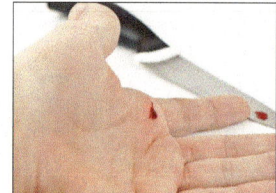

Both *should* and *have to* can be used to give strong advice.

Should	Really Should	Have to
- is often used when asking for advice. *I cut myself. What should I do?*	- *really* is used to make the advice stronger. *You really should wash it out with soap.*	- is stronger than *should* and means you don't have a choice. *You have to go to the doctor. The cut looks deep.*

PART 2

Discuss the situations with a partner.

❶ What does Jon have to do?

He really should...

He has to...

❷ What should Jan do?

She really should...

She has to...

3 **What should Dan do?**

He really should...

He has to...

He really should...

4 **What should Kip do?**

He has to...

5 **What should Sam do?**

She has to...

She really should...

Unit 7 Give Me a Hint | 143

B. Psychobabble

PART 1 • Take turns playing the role of a doctor and a patient. As the patient, tell your doctor about some of the problems you are having. Your partner will give you advice to help solve the problem.

> **Example: You can't stop eating ice cream.**
> **A:** *I can't stop eating ice cream.*
> **B:** *You have to try bacon ice cream. It's delicious!*

STUDENT A Patient Issues

- You can't stop eating ice cream.
- Every time you hear music, you have to start dancing.
- Every time you use the Internet, you start crying.
- You think you're a cat.
- You wish you were still in high school.
- You think you were **abducted** by aliens.

STUDENT B Patient Issues

- You are hearing voices in your head.
- You can't **get over** your last relationship.
- You can't understand the emotions of others. For example, when people are happy, you think they are sad; when they are sad, you think they are happy.
- You think your partner is trying to kill you.
- You think you're in a dream and you can't wake up.
- You are addicted to shopping.

PART 2 • Report to the class how the Doctor solved your problems.

> **Example: You can't stop eating ice cream.**
> **B:** *The doctor said I had to try bacon ice cream because it's delicious.*

Abduct (v.): to take someone away by force
Get over (phrasal v.): recover from

C. The Amazing Adventures of

THE THREE STARS DETECTIVE AGENCY

Billy the Magician Policeman
Bonus: Can choose both choices once

Marie the Boxing Scientist
Gets a bonus clue (extra point)

Zesty the Famous Chef
Can change choice once

You and your partner(s) are proud members of the Three Stars Detective Agency. Choose one of three detectives to help you solve the Mystery of the Missing Necklace!

STEP 1 In your group, choose one detective to help you!

CLUE

Day 1
- **a.** She doesn't have any enemies. She and her brother are good people!
- **b.** It was her father's necklace. He was a magician. +1 Clue

Day 2
- **a.** You find a burnt flier for the circus. A hand written note signed –"RF" +1 Clue
- **b.** A neighbor saw a mean gang of clowns watching the apartment.

Day 3
- **a.** You beat the Strong Man! He tells you "RF" might mean Red Flag – he was a magician who worked here, but he was fired. He was always angry and scared the customers. +1 Clue
- **b.** You **escape** the circus!

Day 4
- **a.** It is a burned piece of paper, " --- will pay for --- father's crimes! -RF" Written on a **flyer** for the Pyramid Theatre. +1 Clue
- **b.** She said she had to meet someone at the Pyramid Theatre.

Day 5
- **a.** He escapes out a back door, but leaves his jacket. You find a box of matches in the pocket. +1 Clue
- **b.** The person at the counter says he usually hangs out at the local club.

Day 6
- **a.** You **beat up** the clowns! One of them says, "He said if we don't beat you, he will beat us!" The Red Flag got away. +1 Clue
- **b.** You hide in a trash can. The mean clowns leave after a few minutes. You smell like trash.

Day 7
- **a.** You find a picture in his pocket. It's a picture of Ms. Blue and Billy Blue as children. There is an older man wearing the necklace. +1 Clue
- **b.** Billy Blue scratched something onto the ground...a riddle! – "RF is where you go to cross an ocean without a boat."

Day 8
- **a.** A worker saw a man in strange clothes and a girl in blue get on a plane to the island of Costa Lotsa. +1 Clue
- **b.** You give money to the pilot. He tells you that a plane just left to the island of Costa Lotsa. He hands you the business card he received.

Day 9
- **a.** They take you to a **factory**, but it's a trap! They are really a gang of mean clowns!
- **b.** You get lost and drive all night, but you find the factory! +1 Clue

Day 10
- **a.** You run after the Red Flag and catch him before he can escape! +1 Clue
- **b.** You untie Ms. Blue and run to safety. The Red Flag escaped! Maybe the police will catch him... +1 Clue

The Results

1 – 2 clues	The Red Flag gets away, free as a bird. Your agency goes out of business.
3 – 4 clues	You aren't able to **prove** anything. The Red Flag goes free!
5 – 6 clues	You are able to put the Red Flag in jail for kidnapping Ms. Blue.
7 – 8 clues	You are able to put the Red Flag in jail for several crimes. He won't be getting out any time soon.
9 – 11 clues	The Red Flag goes to jail for a long time, you find the stolen necklace, and your stories are turned into a popular book series.

Escape (*v.*): to get free
Factory (*n.*): a building where things are made
Beat up (phrasal *v.*): to injure someone by fighting them
Prove (*v.*): provide evidence for the truth

Discussion Questions

1. Do you often ask people for advice?
   - Do you usually listen to people's advice or ignore it?

2. Who is your favorite person to ask for advice. Why?
   - Is there a problem in your life now that you need advice for?

3. Did you ever give a friend advice and he/she did not listen to you?
   - What happened?

4. Do you often talk to your parents about your problems?
   - Do you prefer to talk to your mother or father about your problems?

5. Do you think the following problems should be solved by yourself or by talking to other people?
   - You need more money.
   - You have problems with your boyfriend/girlfriend.
   - You are getting bad grades in school.

6. If you found out your best friend was going to **therapy**, would you feel surprised?
   - Would you ever go to therapy? Why or why not?

7. What are your favorite mystery stories?

UNIT 7 REVIEW

How well can you use…
- ☐ Ways to express purpose?
- ☐ Different ways to express necessity?

What do you need to study more?

Therapy (n.): treatment of mental problems

Activity: How Many Ways...?

Look at the images below and think of at least three uses for each item.

Example: Tray

You could use it to carry food.
You could use it to keep dry if it rains.
You could use it to protect yourself if you are attacked.

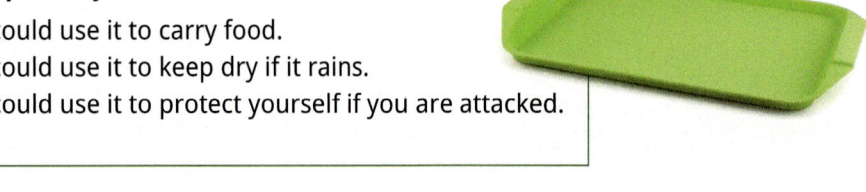

String

Fake mustache

Thimble

Horse shoe

Glass jar

Chick

Snippers

Spring

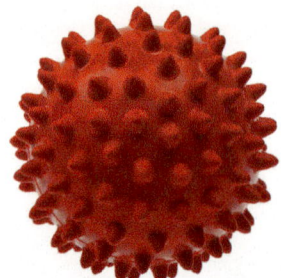
Ball

Segue

Hi there, blogosphere!
I'm Henry Jones, and I like thinking of ways to make life easier. My grandkids are always surprised at the things I come up with, so I started this blog to share them with you.

September 10th Study Tips
Here are some study tips I recently gave my grandson Nick:
• Taking a quick nap after learning something new helps you to remember it better.
• You will remember something easier if you say it out loud than if you read it over and over.

August 1st Health
My youngest grandchild, Bobby, is on summer break. That means lots of bug bites and scraped knees:
• Put scotch tape on a mosquito bite. The itch will stop.
• When you get burned, apply toothpaste. It stops the burning and reduces the pain.

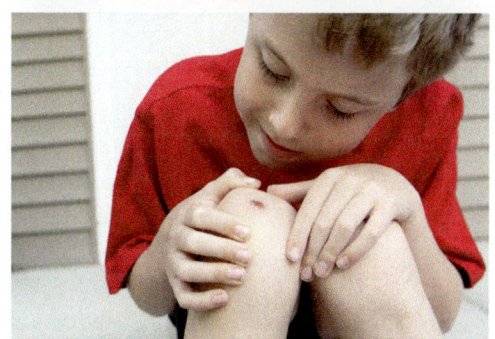

July 20th Appearance
My granddaughter Ella is the most beautiful girl in the world, but she's always worried about her appearance:
• Eating salmon can help your hair grow faster.
• 15 minutes of laughter has the same benefit as 30 minutes of exercise.

A. Discussion
1. Which of the life tips from above did you know before?
   ▶ Which ones surprised you?
2. Do you think any of these tips could be useful to you in life? Why or why not?

B. Writing
Think of a tip you can add to each of the blog entries above. Share what you wrote with your fellow students, and be prepared to explain why your tips work!

08 Taking It All In
The Senses

Objectives:
/ Talk about the five senses
/ Practice using the verbs *listen to* and *hear*

WARM UP

- What are the five senses?
- Rank them in order of most important to least important.
- Which sense is your strongest?
- Which sense is your weakest?

TONGUE TWISTERS

- I see he sees the high seas she sees.
- Sounding by sound is a sound way of sounding sounds.

LESSON 1

A. Tasty/Smelly

TASTE

PART 1

Match each item below to the adjective that describes how it tastes.
What other things can you think of that you like or don't like that taste that way?

- Bitter
- Bland
- Spicy
- Sour
- Salty
- Sweet

Gum drop

Pepper

Cracker

Potato chip

Lemon

Coffee

PART 2

1 Which adjectives best describe food from your country?
2 What's the best _____ food?
3 If your food is _____, what can you do to change it?
4 What is the worst thing you have ever tasted?
5 What is your favorite flavor of ice cream?

Bitter (*adj.*): strong and sharp taste

SMELL

PART 3

Match each item below to the adjective that describes how it smells.

What other things can you think of that you like or don't like that smell that way?

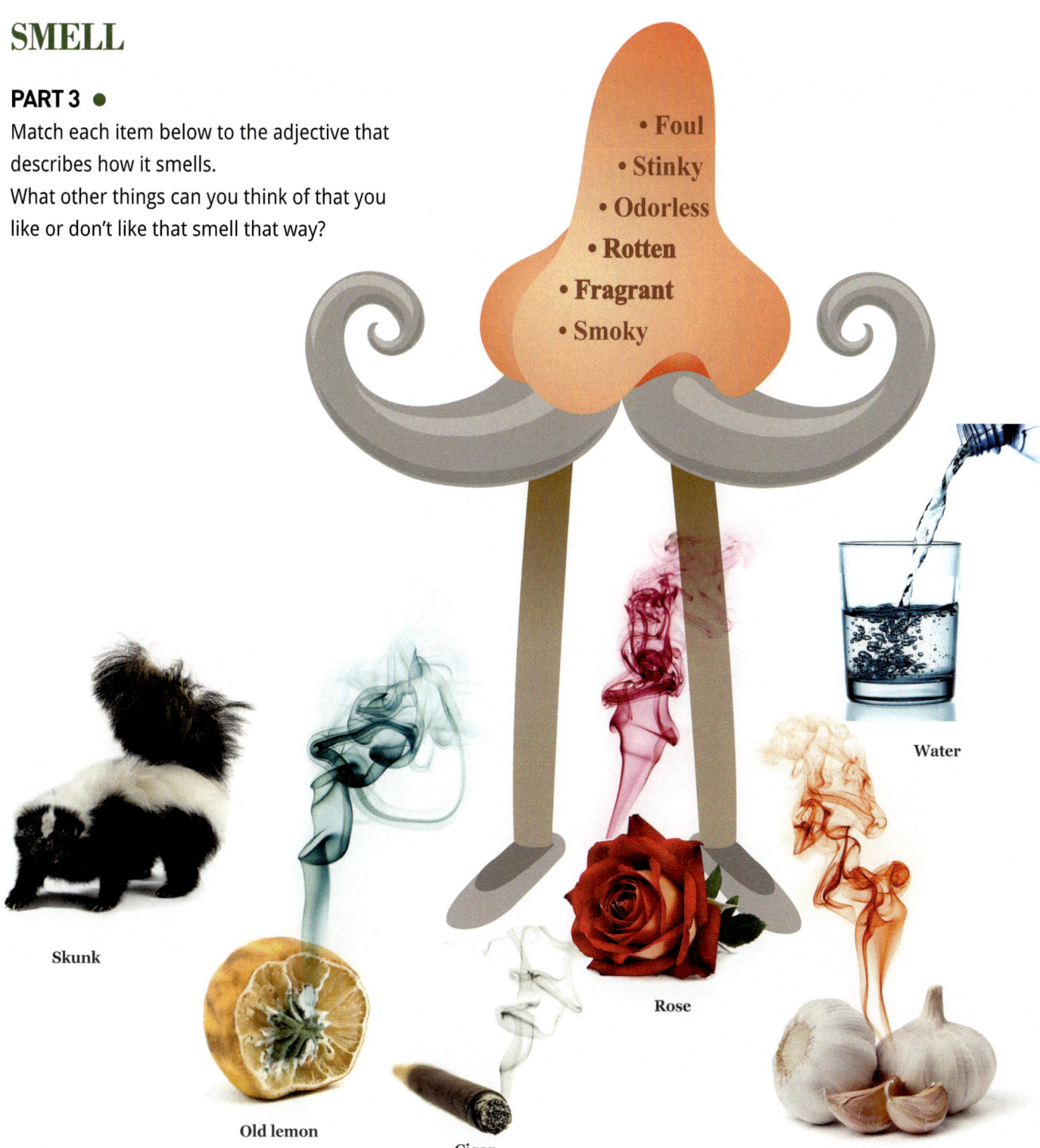

- Foul
- Stinky
- Odorless
- **Rotten**
- **Fragrant**
- Smoky

Skunk

Old lemon

Cigar

Rose

Water

Garlic

PART 4

1 Does your breath smell bad? What can you do if someone's breath smells bad?
2 What are the scents in your house? In your city?
3 Do some smells remind you of a moment in your past?
4 Which bad smells do you **secretly** like?
5 What is the worst thing you have ever smelled?

Rotten (*adj.*): affected by decay
Fragrant (*adj.*): having a pleasant smell
Secretly (*adv.*): not known to others

Unit 8 Taking It All In | 155

B. Noisy/Squeaky

PART 1 •

Pre-listening

Match each item below to the adjective that describes how it sounds. What other things can you think of that sound similar?

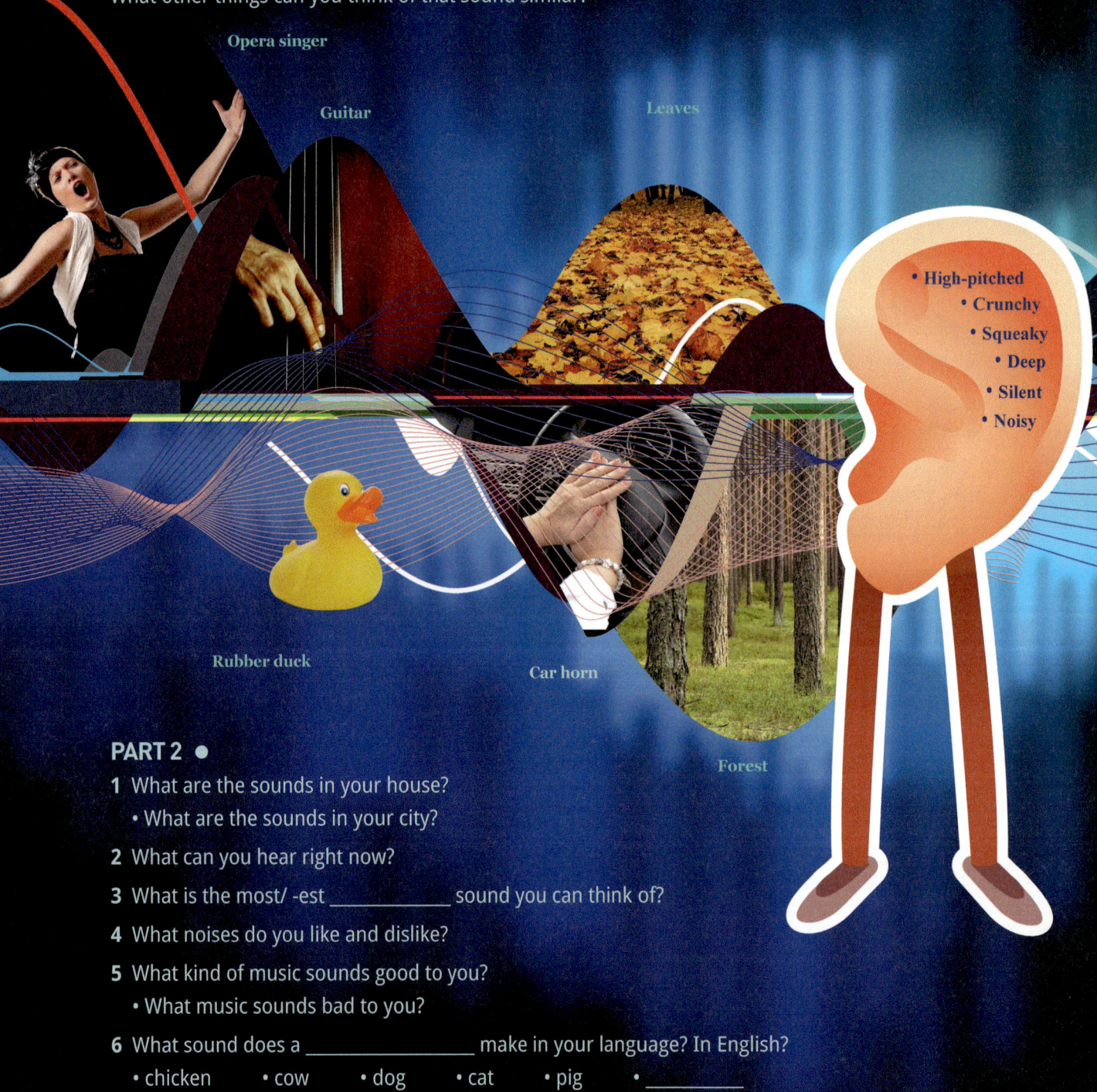

- Opera singer
- Guitar
- Leaves
- Rubber duck
- Car horn
- Forest

- High-pitched
- Crunchy
- Squeaky
- Deep
- Silent
- Noisy

PART 2 •

1. What are the sounds in your house?
   • What are the sounds in your city?
2. What can you hear right now?
3. What is the most/ -est _____ sound you can think of?
4. What noises do you like and dislike?
5. What kind of music sounds good to you?
   • What music sounds bad to you?
6. What sound does a _____ make in your language? In English?
   • chicken   • cow   • dog   • cat   • pig   • _____

Crunchy (*adj.*): makes a loud noise when broken
Squeaky (*adj.*): makes a high noise when pressed

Listening TRACK 16-17

Heather and David wake up in the middle of the night when they hear something downstairs! With a partner, put the pictures in order. Then listen to check if you are correct.

Nick apologizes.

Heather hears something.

Nick eats the cereal.

Nick makes a pot of tea.

Heather and David surprise Nick.

Nick opens a cabinet to get cereal.

Post-listening

Language Point : *Listen to* vs. *Hear*

Listen (to) is used to say that you are paying attention to a sound.

A: *What are you doing?*
B: *I'm listening to the new Crimson Kings album. It's terrible!*

Hear is used to say that you just noticed the sound. You weren't concentrating on anything specifically.

A: *Did you hear that?*
B: *I did. I don't think we're alone in here.*

Describe what you think the people in the pictures *hear* or are *listening to*.
Also, describe what kind of sound you think it is. (noisy, squeaky, etc.)

Darla and Derek are newlyweds.
1 What is Darla listening to?

James works in a factory.
2 What sounds does James hear?

Super Girls are having a concert.
3 What are the fans listening to?

Jonathan is feeding the seagulls.
4 What sounds does Jonathan hear?

Greg is giving a great presentation.
5 What does Greg hear when he finishes?

Mr. Keeper is collecting honey.
6 What sounds can Mr. Keeper hear?

C. Nonsense

What do you sense from the following pictures?
> Is it good or bad?
> Then, describe what you might smell, taste, or hear in this situation.

1. In an elevator

What do you hear when the elevator is empty?
What do you listen to when it's full?
(Another Question)?

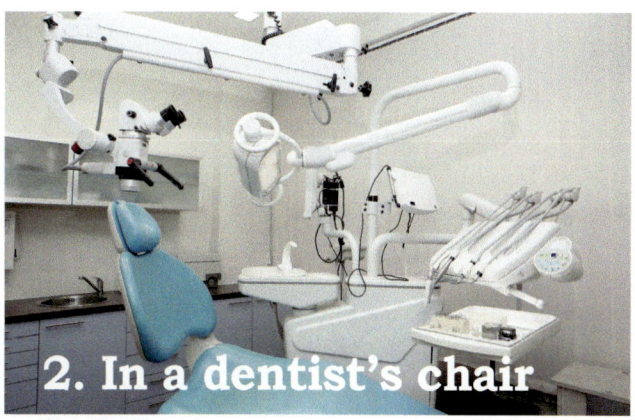

2. In a dentist's chair

What sounds do you hear?
What do you taste?
(Another Question)?

3. In an old basement

What things do you hear?
What things do you smell?
(Another Question)?

4. At the beach

What sounds would you listen to?
How does the ocean taste?
(Another Question)?

5. At a floating market

What can you hear?
What things would you like to taste?
(Another Question)?

6. On a long flight

What do you hear in this situation?
What things do you smell?
(Another Question)?

7. On a cold winter morning

What are you listening to while walking?
How does the air smell?
(Another Question)?

8. Inside a boxing gym

What do you hear in the gym?
How does the gym smell?
(Another Question)?

9. At an outdoor BBQ

How does the meat smell?
What do you think it tastes like?
(Another Question)?

Discussion **Questions**

1 What are the five senses again?
- ▶ What body parts are associated with each sense?

2 What is a nice thing to hear?
- ▶ What is a nice thing to listen to?

3 What do you like to taste?
- ▶ What has a terrible taste?

4 What do you like to smell?
- ▶ How are smell and taste connected?

5 Which sense gives us the most pleasure?
- ▶ If you had to lose one sense, which sense would you lose?

6 Can you feel someone is close to you without seeing, smelling,
- ▶ Which of your senses is the most sensitive?

7 Is there a sixth sense?
- ▶ If yes, do you think you have a sixth sense?

LESSON 2

>> WARM UP

Objectives:
/ Practice using verbs *see*, *watch*, and *look at*
/ Talk about the five senses

Optical Illusion
Which image do you see first? Which second?

A. Now You See Me, Now You Don't

Language Point : *See* vs. *Watch* vs. *Look at*

SEE

See is used to describe what happens when you open your eyes.

A: *What did you see on your hike yesterday?*
B: *I saw a fox chasing a rabbit!*

It is also used when talking about **events** such as a movie, play, or sporting competition.

I'm going to see a baseball game tonight.

LOOK AT

Look at is used when you are focusing on something for a short time.

You are focusing on the thing, not the action.

We looked at several apartments before we decided to buy.

WATCH

Watch is used to show that we are focusing on something for a long time.

I watched TV for three hours last night.

PART 1

Answer the questions using *see*, *look at*, and *watch*.

1. What TV shows do you like to watch?
2. What was the last movie you saw?
3. How often do you look at your phone?
4. When are you going to see your best friend next?
5. Do you ever have to watch a younger family member? Do you like it?
6. What can you see outside of the window?
7. Look at page _____ in the book. What do you see?
8. What is something you never want to see?
9. Do you like to **people watch**?
10. Has anyone ever looked at you and thought you were someone else?

People watch (*idiom*): observing people and their interactions in a casual way

PART 2 Choose a verb, and ask your partner the question. Sometimes either verb is okay.

1 What is he _____? (seeing/watching)
2 What other things is he _____ ?
    (seeing/looking at)

3 What do you ___ the golfer doing?
    (see/look at)
4 What is he   ____? (watching/seeing)

7 What is the man in back ___? (seeing/watching)
8 Who is the man in front ___? (looking at/seeing)

5 What is the man on the left _____? (looking at/seeing)

6 What didn't the man on the left _____? (see/watch)

9 What did the people in the audience come to ____? (see/look at)

10 What is the model _____ ? (looking at/watching)

11 What does the bull _____? (see/look at)

12 What is the man _____? (watching/looking at)

B. Touchy/Feely

PART 1 • Look at the adjectives below that describe touch. With a partner, brainstorm as many things as you can that are...

PART 2 •

1 What is the **texture** of your favorite food?
2 What's the best _____ food?
3 Is there a food you don't like because of its texture?
4 What things other than food feel _____ ?
5 What texture represents your personality?
6 Are you **ticklish**?
  • Do you like being tickled? Why or why not?
7 What gives you **goose bumps**?
8 Do you prefer your pillows to be soft or hard?
9 You just stepped on something _____. What was it?
10 What is the nicest thing to touch?
   • What is the worst thing to touch?

Texture (*n.*): the feel of a surface
Ticklish (*adj.*): sensitive to being touched
Goose bumps (*idiom*): temporary bumps on the skin from cold or fear

C. Sensory Guess What

Choose an item on the next page, but don't tell your partner which one.
He/she must ask sense questions to guess which item it is.

Does it smell…?
Does it feel…?
Does it sound…?
Does it taste …?

Discussion Questions

1. Which do you like more: man-made sounds or sounds in nature?
   - What is your favorite sound in nature?

2. Which sense gives you the most **pleasure**?
   - What things do you enjoy the most with that sense?

3. Are you a **sensitive** person?
   - Which of your senses is the most sensitive? (smell, hearing, etc.)

4. Do you have good vision or do you wear glasses/contact lenses?
   - If you have bad vision, would you consider getting LASIK surgery for your eyes?

5. What do you notice when you first meet a new person? (face, height, etc.)
   - Which part of you do you think is the most attractive? (eyes, nose, hair, hands, etc.)

6. If you had to lose one sense, which one would you lose?
   - If you could only have two senses, which ones would you keep?

7. Many animals and insects have better senses than us. If you could have any animal or insect's sense, which would you have? (For example, a dog's sense of smell, a bat's sense of hearing, etc.)
   - How would you use that sense?

UNIT 8 REVIEW

How well can you use…
- ☐ Adjectives that describe sense?
- ☐ Difficult verbs for listening and seeing?

What do you need to study more?

Pleasure (*n.*): happiness and satisfaction
Sensitive (*adj.*): easy to feel something

Sight
Sound
Smell
Taste
Feel

Activity : Sense Poem

Write a single sentence for each sense to make a poem about a topic. Each line will connect to the sense listed. You can choose the senses in any order.

Example topics: A celebration or holiday, a season, your home town or favorite place, etc.

My Birthday

Friends all laughing and singing songs, (Sound)

Lots of gifts and a chocolate cake. (Sight)

The smell of steak cooking on a grill, (Smell)

A little spicy, the way I like it. (Taste)

Then I sleep in my soft bed. (Feel)

A. Discussion
1. Which of these sound effects surprised you? Do you know any other ways to make sound effects?
2. What sounds can you make just using your mouth, hands, etc.? Make a sound and have your partner try to guess what it is.

B. Writing
Write a very short dialogue including the sound effects above (or use your own).

09
What Seems to Be the Problem?

Problems & Solutions

Objectives:
/ Express that something is more than needed
/ Ask about problems and express complaints

WARM UP

**Which of these things are serious problems, and which are not?
Can you think of any other "serious" problems?**

- Cold drink got warm
- Too many clothes, but nothing to wear
- Bed is too soft
- TV remote is too far away
- Have to change password again
- Left phone charger at work
- Missed the movie previews
- Restaurant messed up my order
- Slept too much
- Elevator is broken, so have to use the stairs

TONGUE TWISTERS

- The problem with the problem is not that it's a problem but that it's probably problematic.

LESSON 1

A. Enough Is Enough

Do You Remember?
Adding *for* or *to* describes purpose.
The weather is hot enough for swimming.
The weather is too cold to swim.

Language Point : Using *Too* and *Enough*

Too: use *Too* to say that something is more than what is needed. It has a negative meaning.
too + adjective: *The weather is too hot.* (I don't like it)
too + adverb: *The teacher spoke too fast.* (I didn't understand)

Enough: use *Enough* to say that something is sufficient.
adjective/adverb + enough: *The weather is hot enough.*

Not enough can express the same meaning as *too*:
The teacher spoke too fast.
→*The teacher did not speak slowly enough.*

PART 1

Answer the following questions using *too* and *enough*.
Try to give a reason why or why not.

Example: *No, I don't think I'm strong enough. An elephant is too big.*

1 Can you lift…
- an elephant?
- a flat screen TV?
- a box of books?
- _____ ?

2 Can you drink…
- a liter of beer?
- a liter of salt water?
- a liter of milk?
- _____ ?

3 Can you run…
- to the bathroom and back?
- to home and back?
- to the ocean and back?
- _____ ?

4 Can you eat…
- half a pizza?
- a whole pizza?
- a chocolate chicken pizza?
- _____ ?

5 How's the weather today? Can you…
- go skiing?
- go swimming?
- go skydiving?
- _____ ?

PART 2

Use *too* and *enough* to describe the following people. Give a reason why you think so.

> **Example: Ralphie wants to go on a trip by himself.**
>
> **A:** *I don't think Ralphie is old enough to travel by himself. And that suitcase looks too heavy.*
>
> **B:** *You're right. He's not old enough to travel by himself, but he's strong enough to carry that suitcase!*

I think Cindy is too…

I don't think Cindy is _____ enough.

Your English teacher wants to teach math.

Cindy wants to be a comedian.

Ralphie wants to go on a trip by himself.

Didi likes these shoes.

Manny wants to join a boy band.

Grandma wants you to pet Sprinkles.

Jerry's going to buy his girlfriend a new cell phone.

B. You Gotta Problem?

Language Point : Asking About and Discussing Problems

▶ What's wrong with…?   *What was wrong with the movie?*
▶ What's the matter with…?   *What was the matter with the movie?*

You can use *not enough* to say there isn't a sufficient amount of something.

Not enough + noun:
The movie didn't have enough action.

You can also use *too much* and *too many* to say there is more than what is necessary.

Too many + count noun:
The movie had too many car chases.

Do You Remember?

many and much
Many is used with count nouns:
hamburgers, cars, computers

Much is used with non-count nouns:
juice, rice, air

Pre-listening

1 Choose a person, place, or thing and ask your partner a question about it.
   A: *What's wrong with English?*

2 Choose a noun to **complain** about, or think of your own. It's okay to say you don't have a problem, but you should give a reason why.

Things:
Television
Computers
The weather
Education
English
This classroom
Other?

Places:
Your school
Your work
Your house
You city
Your country
The planet

People:
Your boss
Your professors
Young people
Old people
Your friends
Your family

Count:
Cars   Computers
Dogs   Cigarettes
Trees   Teachers
Taxes   Bosses
Insects   Other?

Non Count:
Traffic   Homework
Sadness   Money
People   Studying
Death   Drinking
Smoke   Other?

B: *Well, there's too much vocabulary. What do you think?*

A: *I think there are too many **exceptions** to grammar rules!*

Complain (v.): to express unhappiness
Exceptions (n.): something not included

Listening TRACK 18-19

Bobby, David, and Heather are discussing which movie to see. They all have different opinions of each other's choices. Choose the nouns and adjectives they use to describe the movies.

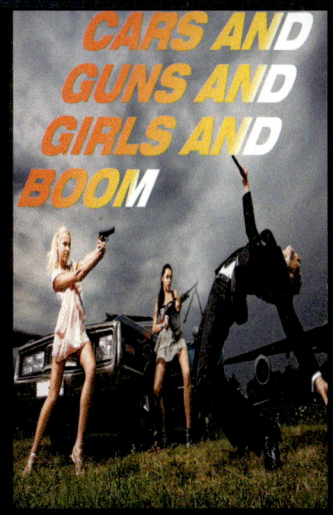

David's choice

Heather's choice

Bobby's Choice

Heather:
There's too much_____.
violence / romance
Bobby:
There's not enough _____.
cars / jokes

David:
There's not enough ____.
action / comedy
Bobby:
There's too much _____.
kissing / singing

Heather:
It's too _____.
silly / serious
David:
Looks _____ enough.
interesting / funny

Post-listening

1 What movie did the family decide on?

2 What movie would you choose?

3 Look at the movie genres.
 • Which ones do you like?
 • Which ones don't you like?
 • What's the matter with them?

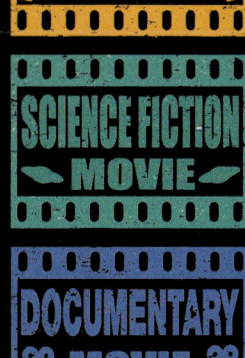

C. The Complaint Department

You and your partner work for the Universal Complaint Department. People call 1-555-COMPLAINT with all of their problems. Respond to their complaints, and offer solutions.

1-1555
Complaint Department

PART 1

Welcome to the Department! You're an intern, so we will start with some easy problems.

1. My hotel room isn't big enough.
2. I went out on a date with a guy… and he left halfway through the meal. He didn't even pay.
3. Hey, we are calling from the hotel again. Our room smells like cigarette smoke.
4. I don't know where to go on vacation. I have too much money and I don't know what to do!
5. We're calling from the hotel one last time. We decided to leave the hotel. Where should we look for a new hotel?

PART 2

Not bad, kid. You earned a promotion! And now you're dealing with some more difficult problems.

1. The rent at my apartment building is way too high! I can barely **afford** it!
2. I think one of the rooms in my apartment complex is on fire…
3. Mayor McMayorsberg here. Yes, I'm sure you're honored. Look, it turns out my popularity is down. Nobody seems to like me enough.
4. My friend said he couldn't **hang out** because he was too busy studying. I found out he was at the bar.
5. There's a person **drowning** in the river, but I can't swim…
6. This is the mayor. Thanks to you, my popularity is up, but now the town is under attack by zombies! There's too many of them. What should we do?!

PART 3

Because you helped the mayor, you've been given your own department! Now things get difficult. You might have to get some help to answer these…

1. Hello? Yeah, my friend was **bitten** by a snake while hiking. Do we have enough time to get to a hospital?
2. Yes, I keep calling the Complaint Department and the advice is too terrible.
3. Hello? Hello? My name is Timmy. I waited all night to see Santa Claus but he never came.
4. Greetings! This is the British people from the year 865 AD. We are being attacked by Viking armies.
5. This is a cat. I have been staring at my human for twenty minutes now, and he hasn't given me what I want.

Promotion (*n.*): advancement in position
Afford (*v.*): to have enough money
Hang out (*phrasal v.*): to spend time together
Drown (*v.*): to die from being covered by water
Bite (*v.*): to tear through the skin with teeth

Discussion Questions

1. Are you busy these days?
   - How much free time do you have?

2. Do you have a lot of stress?
   - What kinds of things stress you out?

3. What are some good and bad things about living in a big city?
   - Do you think you could live in the countryside? Why or why not?

4. What are some things you don't like about…
   …your job?
   …your boyfriend/girlfriend or husband/wife?
   …your country?

5. Have you ever returned an item to a store?
   - What was the problem with the item?

6. Can you remember the last time you were unhappy with the service at a restaurant or store?
   - Did you do anything about it?
   - Did you talk to the manager of the restaurant or store?

7. Where is a place you visited that was too…
   - …crowded?
   - …dirty?
   - …boring?
   - …old?

LESSON 2

>> WARM UP

Objectives:
/ Express displeasure
/ Talk about ways to fix problems

My Bad

What do you do if you hurt the feelings of…

- your mom?
- your enemy?
- your pet?
- your teacher?
- your best friend?
- a **telemarketer**?
- a stranger on the subway?
- your boyfriend/girlfriend/husband/wife?

I would probably…

Apologize and buy him/her a gift.
Say sorry politely, but not really care.
Laugh and laugh.
Ignore him/her until they say something.
Send a text saying I'm sorry.
Never speak to him/her again.
Not even care.
(Other)

Telemarketer (n.): a person who sells things over the phone

A. The Answer Is "No"

Language Point: Ways To Say No

There are many ways to say no.
Some sound more formal than others.

◄───►
Direct   **Polite**

Are you kidding me?   **No way!**   **No.**   **I don't think so.**   **I'm sorry, but no.**

Below are a series of questions you probably want to answer "Yes" to. But, your job is to answer, "No", and give a good reason why you do not want it.

1 Do you want this delicious cake?

> **Example:**
>
> *I'm sorry, but no. It looks too delicious.
> I have to eat these carrots right now.*

2 Do you want to have a family?
3 Do you want to speak perfect English without studying?
4 Would you like a brand new smartphone for free?
5 Would you like me to pay for lunch?
6 Are you going to pick that money up off the ground?
7 Do you want to marry the man/woman of your dreams?
8 Are you happy that it's your birthday?
9 Would you like to be able to eat whatever you want without getting fat?
10 Is class over?
11 Should I give you a foot massage?
12 Do you like getting presents?
13 Would you like some more dessert?
14 Do you want to go to your favorite restaurant for dinner?
15 Do you want to get ice cream instead of going to the dentist?
16 Should I give you a raise for your hard work?
17 Can I buy you these new shoes?
18 Can I give you a compliment?

B. Problem Solved

· could, should, why don't we for making recommendations.

> First choose a role in the group (A, B, C, or D).
> This will be your role for each situation. In each situation you have a problem or something you want.
> See if you can make a **compromise** as a group.

You and your team members are....

1 A family: You have to decide what do together on "family day".

A. Dad
- I want to see a romantic comedy.
- I don't want to do anything too expensive.

B. Mom
- I want to go to a Formula One race.
- We don't get enough excitement.

C. Junior
- I have too much homework. I can't go out for long.
- I feel like going to the library.

D. Gemma
- No one ever listens to me!
- Why don't we go to the mall?

Compromise (*n.*): an agreement between two or more people
Atmosphere (*n.*): the way in which a place feels

182 | SLE Generations 1B

2 Friends going out to eat

A. Carol
- I want to go out for sushi.
- I don't like to eat anything too greasy.

B. Liz
- I would like to eat something spicy.
- I don't like restaurants that are too crowded.

C. Gwen
- I'm really into creamy pasta.
- I want to go to a restaurant that's popular.

D. Mary
- We should go somewhere with good music and **atmosphere**.
- I'm not hungry enough for a big meal.

3 A Study Group: You have a class project to design a concept for a new smartphone app.

A. Kris
- We could make an app that helps kids study.
- There are too many games already.

B. Keith
- I don't think most apps are exciting enough.
- I want to make an app that tells you where the party is!

C. Steph
- Why don't we design an app that teaches people how to dance?
- People spend too much time just looking at their phones.

D. Steve
- Thinking of something ourselves is too difficult.
- We should call my cousin. His job is making apps.

Unit 9 What Seems to Be the Problem? | 183

C. Forgive, Forget, Revenge

Your partner(s) did something horrible to you. Will you forgive and forget, or get revenge?

Step 1
- Read the box, and tell your partner(s) what you think of the situation.
  How does the situation make you feel?

Step 2
Now, decide what you will do:

Forgive: If you forgive your partner(s), you get **1** point. Tell your partner why you would forgive him/her.
I would forgive you because...

Revenge: If you want revenge, tell your partner(s) why.
I want revenge because...

Step 3

Now, flip a coin. Then, check the revenge table on page 186 to see what happens.
- Heads means you win. Read the *Success!* to your partner(s). You get **2** points!
- Tails means you lose. Your **partner** reads the *Backfire!* to you. **0** points.

Example: You called your partner but they didn't answer the phone.

A: *I don't think that's a very big problem. I would forgive you. Maybe you were busy.*

B: *I want revenge because I think that is really rude! You should not ignore phone calls.*

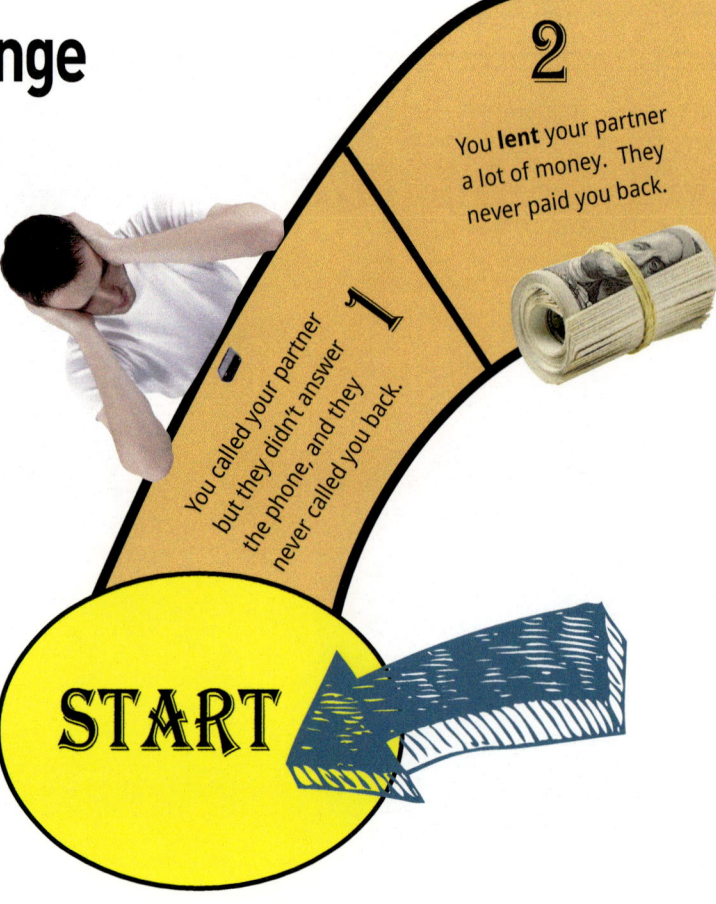

1. You called your partner but they didn't answer the phone, and they never called you back.

2. You **lent** your partner a lot of money. They never paid you back.

START

	POINTS
1.	
2.	
3.	
4.	
5.	
6.	
7.	
8.	
9.	
10.	
11.	
12.	
Total	

Backfire (*v.*): an attempt that fails
Lend (*v.*): to give something for a short time
Borrow (*v.*): to take something for a short time
Apply (*v.*): formally request something

REVENGE TABLE

The Revenge	Heads – Success!	Tails – Backfire!
1. You put your partner's phone number on the Internet.	You say it's the number of a famous celebrity. Now he/she gets hundreds of calls a day!	Your partner becomes an internet celebrity!
2. Your cousin says he can hack into your partner's bank account.	Your cousin transfers the money to you. And a little extra. Nice.	Your cousin accidentally transfers all of your money into your partner's account. Ouch.
3. Your partner asks you to give them the answer on the test...	You give him/her the wrong answers.	You give your partner the wrong answer but he/she still gets a better score than you.
4. You go on vacation...	You bring your partner back a cursed monkey head. He/she has bad luck forever.	You bring your partner back the ugliest souvenir you can find. You find out later that it is actually worth a lot of money.
5. You ask to borrow your partner's phone.	You "accidentally" drop it. The screen breaks.	You "accidentally" drop it and break your toe. The phone is okay.
6. You order another coffee.	You spill it on their lap.	But your partner drinks that one, too.
7. You decide to embarrass your friend.	You tell an embarrassing story about your partner and everyone laughs.	You tell an embarrassing story about your partner and everyone thinks it's cute.
8. On their birthday, you give him/her a gift card...	It's the same gift card he/she gave you... but it is now expired.	When your partner takes the gift card to buy ice cream, they are the 1,000,000th customer. They win ice cream for life.
9. You yell at your partner.	Your partner is embarrassed and everyone makes him/her go to the back of the line.	The police take you away for making too much noise.
10. When they drive off...	You call the police and tell them the car is stolen.	You throw your shoe at the car and lose the shoe.
11. You call the company and say bad things about him/her.	Your partner's new boss fires him/her.	They don't believe you and give your partner a promotion.
12. You tell your partner he/she has very bad manners.	Your partner runs away crying.	After your partner leaves, you find a note thanking you very much for the delicious meal.

Discussion Questions

1 If someone is mad or sad because of you, do you try to explain yourself?
   ▶ Are you always honest when you explain?

2 Are you a "yes" person or a "no" person?
   ▶ Do you have trouble saying "no"?

3 What's your favorite revenge movie? Why do you like it?
   ▶ Why do you think movies about revenge are so popular?

4 Talk about a time when you forgave somebody for something.
   ▶ What happened after you forgave the person?

5 Would you forgive someone for:
   ▶ Stepping on your shoes?
   ▶ Hitting your pet with their car?
   ▶ Stealing your wallet/purse?
   ▶ Spilling coffee on your computer?

6 Do you prefer working on a project in a group or by yourself?

UNIT 9 REVIEW

How well can you use…
☐ Ways to express complaints?
☐ Expressions for saying "No"?
What do you need to study more?

Activity: Solutions

Look at the solutions below and make up what the problem was.

1 Take some medicine.
2 Change my password.
3 **Buy her a kitten.**
4 **Take an English class.**
5 Go to the grocery store.
6 **Hit him!**
7 **Apologize and send flowers.**
8 Join a gym.
9 Promise not to tell anyone.
10 **Write it down so you don't forget next time.**
11 **A fish.**
12 Pretend you didn't notice.

Now make up your own solution and have your partners make up a problem!

SHORTFLICKS.COM

Movie reviews in 15 words or less:

The Tears of a Clown

Joe C. says:
It was so touching. I looked around at the end, and everyone was crying.

Katie P. says:
This movie was way too sentimental. The story was so bad it made me cry.

Gina K. says:
I would watch this movie every day if I could, but I don't have a boyfriend.

Cars and Guns and Girls and Boom

Gabe Y. says:
If you only see one movie again, it should be this one!

Maria K says:
Plenty of sexy girls, but definitely not enough sexy guys! Louder than bombs.

Lilith F. says:
Why are all action movies violent? Too many cars, guns, girls, and boom for me.

Bear in a Boat

Bobby J says:
The only thing wrong with this movie was that it ended too fast!

Heather J says:
Bear in a Boat? The lead actor is a real animal!

David J says:
Too many shots of the bear in stormy seas. Made me a little sea sick.

A. Discussion

1. How did each of the people above feel about the movie he/she saw?
   ▸ Did he/she like it or dislike it?
2. Do you trust professional movie reviewers, or do you prefer to get recommendations from your friends?

B. Writing

Think of the last three movies you saw. Write a fifteen word review for each one.

WARM UP

SELF EVALUATION:
Look at the list of topics and skills we studied.
Which topics and skills did you improve? = √
Which skills do you need to study more? = O
Which skills do you not know? = X

Unit 1 Don't I Know You?
☐ Asking for more information   √ O X
☐ Asking about what was said   √ O X

Unit 2 Wish You Were Here
☐ Giving your opinion   √ O X
☐ Making informal suggestions   √ O X

Unit 3 The Human Environment
☐ Comparing things   √ O X
☐ Describing distance   √ O X

Unit 4 Frequently Asked Questions
☐ Describing how often you do things   √ O X
☐ Expressing preferences   √ O X

Unit 5 Where Were You When
☐ Describing when things happen   √ O X
☐ Asking about what happened next   √ O X

Unit 6 Mixed Feelings
☐ Asking about and describing feelings   √ O X
☐ Expressing possibility with *would*   √ O X

Unit 7 Give Me a Hint
☐ Describing purpose with *used to* and *used for*   √ O X
☐ Giving strong advice and showing necessity   √ O X

Unit 8 Taking It All In
☐ Describing senses
☐ Using difficult verbs for sound and sight

Unit 9 What Seems to Be the Problem?
☐ Using *too* and *enough*
☐ Ways to say "no"

Evaluation
√ = 3 points
O = 2 points
X = 1 point

42-54 points: Ready for the next level, 1C.
30-42 points: Maybe stay in 1B one more month to improve.
18-30 points: Need to study 1B again.

Unit 10 Looking Back | 191

LESSON 1

A. Believe It or Not!

Take turns with your classmates asking each other for explanations for the following situations. When answering, try to think of a few different possibilities.

1. John and Helen got divorced. Why...?

   Ex. *I think Jon was having lunch with his ex-girlfriend when Helen saw them together.*

2. Joan is depressed. Why...?

3. Peter is in jail. Why...?

4. Paul yelled at his son. Why...?

5. Lisa and her mom had a terrible fight last night. Why...?

6. John didn't go to college. Why...?

7. Joanne quit her job. Why...?

8. Michael is in a really bad mood today. Why...?

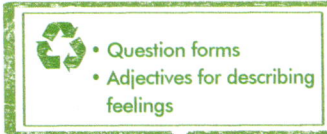
- Question forms
- Adjectives for describing feelings

9. Bob is going to Europe. Why…?

10. Ernie is drinking beer. Why…?

11. It is midnight, and Mike is still working. Why…?

12. A policeman is chasing a man. Why…?

13. Helen is lying on the kitchen floor. Why…?

14. Robert is hiding in a closet. Why…?

15. Bill made a lot of money. How…?

16. Henry lived to be 100 years old. How…?

17. They were friends, but they became enemies. How…?

18. Emily reads three books a week. How…?

19. Wolfgang is a fabulous pianist. How…?

20. Brad is world famous. How…?

B. Meet the New Neighbors

• expressing possibility using could

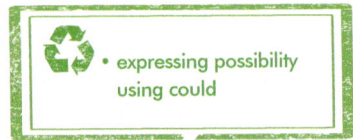

Pre-listening

Imagine that you are moving into a new house.

1 Where would your new house be located?
2 What color would you like to paint your house?
3 Would you have a pet?
4 Which famous person would you like to be your neighbor?

Listening

TRACK 20-21

Three different families moved in across the street from the Jones' house. Heather met them, but can't remember which house they live in, and what pets they have. Listen, and circle the things Heather says about each neighbor.

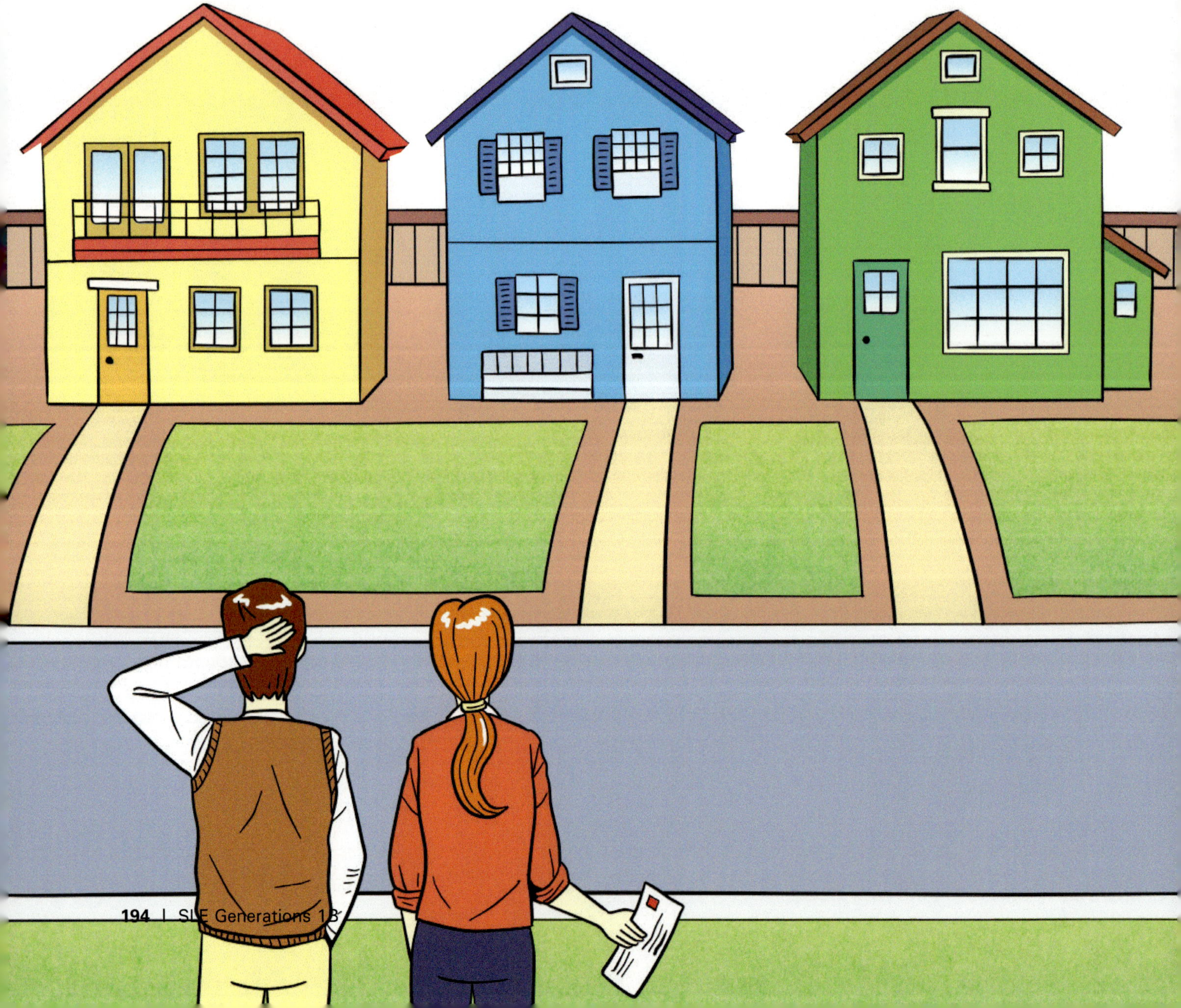

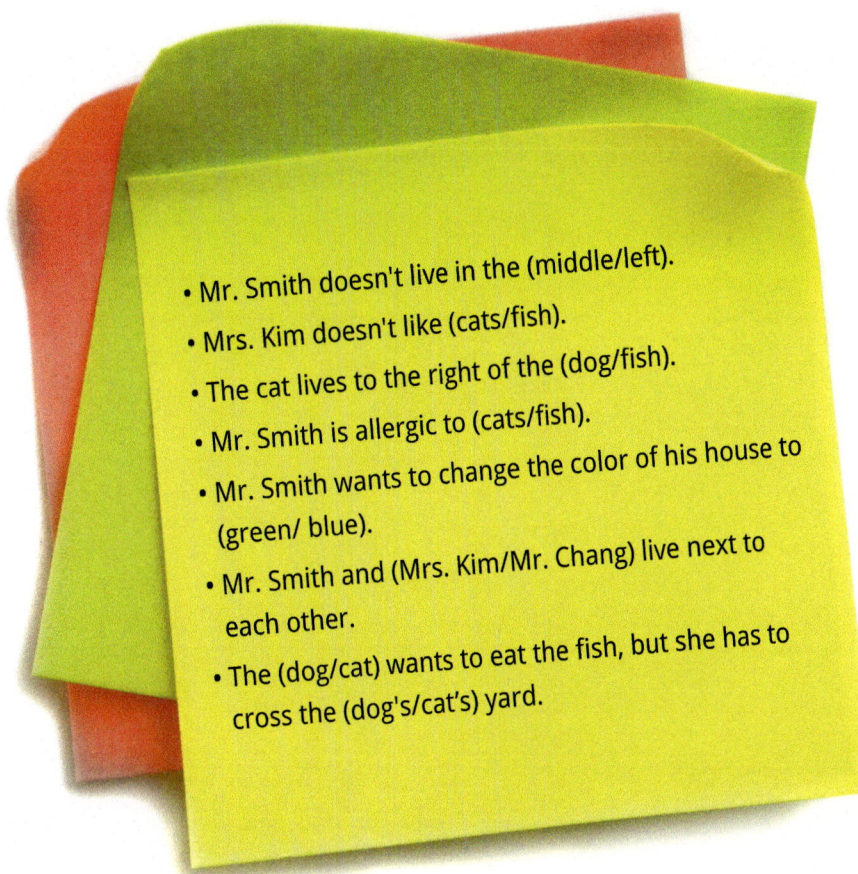

- Mr. Smith doesn't live in the (middle/left).
- Mrs. Kim doesn't like (cats/fish).
- The cat lives to the right of the (dog/fish).
- Mr. Smith is allergic to (cats/fish).
- Mr. Smith wants to change the color of his house to (green/ blue).
- Mr. Smith and (Mrs. Kim/Mr. Chang) live next to each other.
- The (dog/cat) wants to eat the fish, but she has to cross the (dog's/cat's) yard.

Post-listening

Using the clues you heard, help David answer the question:
Who lives in each house, and what pets do they have? (Hint: Put an **X** in the boxes you know are not the answer, and an **O** in the boxes that are.)

	Yellow	Blue	Green	Cat	Fish	Dog
Mr. Chang						
Mr. Smith						
Mrs. Kim						
Cat						
Fish						
Dog						

Person	House	Pet
Mr. Chang		
Mr. Smith		
Mrs. Kim		

C. Comedy of Errors

- Divide into teams.
- One team flips a coin to move a square.
- After landing on a space, correct the sentence.
- A correct answer is worth 2 points.
- The next team flips a coin to move forward. The team with the most points at the end of the game wins!

START	Who is your name?	An orange this is?	What is flirt meaning?	He said he goes on a trip.	I don't liking chocolate.
Or we will could eat at Josie's.	Why doesn't we eat at Joe's?	I play swimming.	Does you think travelling is important?	Do you want to go shopping or to go skating?	I hated vegetables, but now I hate them.
How much apples is there?	This house is biggest than that house.	Her house is most bigger.	There are books in the table.	He is brown eyes.	My house is far to the school.
I wake up early at the morning.	She are eating a hamburger.	I brush three time a day.	How often brush your teeth?	Can you holding your breath for one minute?	Our city is not as big your city.
When I arrive, He was study.	I feel boring.	Would you is happy lying on the beach?	I was seeing TV last night.	The weather is enough hot for swimming.	FINISH

D. Second Worst Hotel Ever

You and your partner traveled a long way for a dream vacation. Unfortunately, when you got to your hotel, things were not what you expected.

Take turns as the customer and the hotel manager, complaining and making excuses for the problems. Then find an alternative solution.

Problems at the Costa Lotsa Hotel & Resort

1. You reserved a luxury suite, but the only room they have is a standard room with one double bed. It is a smoking room.
2. The hotel said, "Free Internet" but it isn't wi-fi, and you have to pay $20 to rent the internet cable.
3. There is a pool, but there is no water in it.
4. Complimentary breakfast buffet? It's just some cereal and room temperature milk.
5. Your neighbors are very loud. They are having a party with lots of people.
6. The sheets are dirty. The hotel already replaced them for you...with more dirty sheets.
7. You asked for an in-room massage. A man named Bruno came, but he was too strong. Now your back hurts so much that you can't walk.

Now, come up with some other possible problems and complain to the hotel manager.

Example: Broken toilet

A: *Excuse me, but the toilet in my room is broken!*

B: *I'm so sorry! It doesn't work because...the last guest broke it. You can use the toilet in the lobby.*

A: *But I want to shower!*

B: *Well, we have a pool...*

Suite (*n.*): set of rooms

E. Tourist Trap

1 Which of these places would you like to visit? Why?

2 Which of these places would you not like to visit? Why?

- using *too* and *enough*
- giving opinions
- making suggestions

Country: Nepal
People: Nepalese
Language: Nepali
Capital: Kathmandu
Sites: Annapurna Trek, Boudhanath Temple

Country: Switzerland
People: Swiss
Language: French, German, Italian
Capital: Bern
Sites: Matterhorn, Lake Geneva

Country: Botswana
People: The Botswana
Language: English, Tswana
Capital: Gaborone
Sites: Okavango Delta, Kalahari Desert

Country: Cuba
People: Cubans
Language: Spanish
Capital: Havana
Sites: Old Havana, Sierra Maestra

Country: Australia
People: Australians
Language: English
Capital: Canberra
Sites: Bondi Beach, Sydney Opera

Country: Cambodia
People: Cambodians
Language: Khmer
Capital: Phnom Penh
Sites: Angkor Wat, Mekong dolphins

3 Choose one country. Which things do you want to do while there?
I could...
- Sleep all day
- Shop
- Sightsee
- Go to discos
- Etc.

Unit 10 Looking Back | 199

4 Now, work with a partner to design a vacation for a friend you met on the vacation from the previous page. He/she is coming to visit you in your city!

A: Where is your friend from?
B: My friend is Swiss. He is from Switzerland. What **should** I do with him?
A: You **have to** take him out for.....
You should...
Why don't you...?

Think of questions to ask for all of these points:
- Location   **ex.** *Where should I take him?*
- Season
- Activities
- Shopping
- Travel partners
- Length of stay
- Weather
- Sightseeing
- Food
- Interesting experiences

F. Freddy Fatso's

PART 1

You and your partner are going out for a meal. Discuss what you will order.

Freddy Fatso's Bar & Grill Menu

Appetizers

Spinach Dip	$3
Potato Skins	$5
Spicy Buffalo Wings	$7
Chicken Nachos	$9

Soups

Broccoli Cheese Soup	$4
Cream of Mushroom Soup	$4

Salads

Grilled Chicken Caesar Salad	$10
Shrimp Salad	$8
Cobb Salad	$6

Hamburgers & Sandwiches

Bacon Cheeseburger	$10
Veggie Burger	$8
Club Sandwich	$7
Chicken Sandwich	$10

Entrees

Fish & Chips	$12
Salmon Steak	$15
Five Cheese Lasagna	$12
Sweet & Sour Pork	$18
New York Strip Steak	$24
Barbeque Ribs	$20

Drinks

Soda	$2
Beer	$4
Wine	$8
Coffee	$4
Tea	$3
Juice	$4

Desserts

Ice Cream	$6
Cheese Cake	$8
Fruit Platter	$10

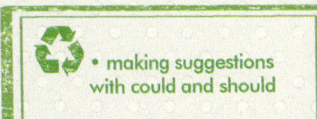
• making suggestions with could and should

Vegetarian (*n.*): a person who does not eat meat
Sweet tooth (*idiom*): really enjoys candy and sweets

PART 2 • Help the following groups plan their meals.

1 Group 1 has a budget of $50 for four people.
2 Group 2 are all **vegetarians**.
3 Group 3 are all on diets.
4 Group 4 has a **sweet tooth**.

G. Best of the Best

PART 1

In pairs or small groups, decide who you think is the "best" and "worst" in each category. Make sure you discuss why you think they deserve to be the best or the worst.

The Categories

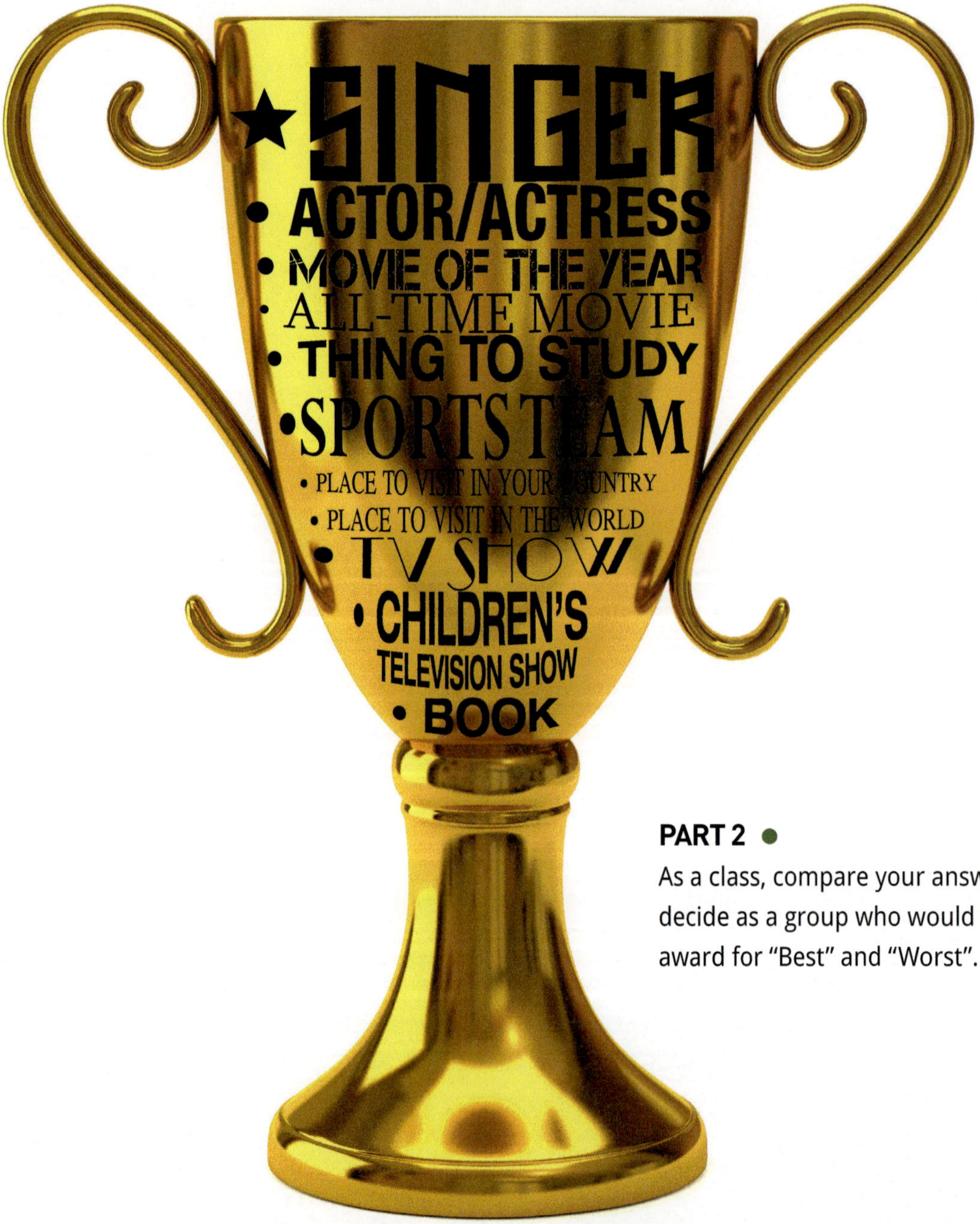

- SINGER
- ACTOR/ACTRESS
- MOVIE OF THE YEAR
- ALL-TIME MOVIE
- THING TO STUDY
- SPORTS TEAM
- PLACE TO VISIT IN YOUR COUNTRY
- PLACE TO VISIT IN THE WORLD
- TV SHOW
- CHILDREN'S TELEVISION SHOW
- BOOK

PART 2

As a class, compare your answers and decide as a group who would win the award for "Best" and "Worst".

H. Review Discussion

First, ask a question about the family. Use the listening scripts in the back of the book to help you answer. Then, ask a question about what you learned.

1. What expression did David's student say when he gets the answer?
2. What does the expression mean?

3. What happened on Grandma Ruth's vacation?
4. What do you suggest I do when I visit your home town?

5. Does Ella want to live in the smallest or the biggest apartment?
6. What is something you like that is far from your house? How about close to your house?

7. How often does Nick have to water the plants?
8. Do you prefer staying in your country or going abroad on vacation?

9. What was Ella doing when Bobby called?
10. What happened the last time you went to dinner?

11. What feeling did Heather say Woofy felt?
12. Would you be happy studying in SLE again?

13. What does Grandpa Henry use the walnut for?
14. What do you have to do to become better at speaking English?

15. What is Nick listening to in the kitchen?
16. What did you see before class today? What did you watch?

17. What movie does Heather say has too much violence?
18. What don't you have enough of in your life?

19. Have you ever lost or broken a phone? How did it happen? What did you do?
20. What is something you might study in 1C?

Activity: Loose Lips

STEP 1

Think of a person. It could be a celebrity, a politician, or even another classmate.

> **Example:** *I've thought of a person!*

STEP 2

Your partners or class will ask questions in the categories on the next page, but do not answer them. Instead, whisper the answer to the person sitting next to you.

> **Example:** *Sue is sitting next to Jill.*
> **Mike:** *I want to know this person's height.*
> **Jill** (*whispers the height to Sue.*)
> **Sue:** *Okay.*
> **Mike:** *Did she say this person is tall?*

STEP 3

Continue whispering answers to the person next to you until the class guesses the person you chose.

> **Example:**
> **Sue:** *No, she didn't say he was tall.*
> **Jason:** *Did she say this person is short?*
> **Sue:** *Yes, she said he's a little short!*

Categories

Height
Weight
Nationality
Job
Gender
Personality
Hair/Eye/Skin Color

LISTENING DIALOGUES SLE 1B

UNIT 1 TRACK 2 and 3

David: How's it going, Daniel?

Daniel: I'm having a lot of difficulty with this problem. I tried solving it using the method in the book, but it keeps coming out wrong.

David: Don't worry, there's more than one way to skin a cat.

Daniel: What do you mean, Mr. Jones?

David: What that means is there is more than one way to solve a problem. Just try changing these two numbers.

Daniel: Wow, Mr. Jones! That makes it really easy. That's the bomb!

David: I'm sorry, Daniel. Did you say "the bomb"?

Daniel: Haha. Ya, Mr. Jones, that means it's really great! Thanks.

UNIT 2 TRACK 4 and 5

Ruth: Hey, friends and family! Grandma Ruth here with my latest podcast from my vacation in beautiful Kipi Kipi. This morning, our travel guide said we could either go hiking or scuba diving. It was very hot, so we went scuba diving! At noon, we had a big lunch – apples, bananas, and some kind of melon. In the afternoon, I rode an elephant across a river! How exciting is that? His name is Earl. Unfortunately, I lost control of Earl and destroyed a few local stores and cafes…so, I'm in jail now. But your grandfather will send money to get me out tomorrow morning. Don't worry, everyone here is nice, and I found a nice souvenir to help me remember my trip! It sure hurt when I got it. Oh well. Until next time, much love, Grandma!

UNIT 3 TRACK 6 and 7

David: How's the apartment search coming, Ella?

Ella: Not bad. I found a few places close to where I want to live.

David: Are they in your price range?

Ella: Well, these two are. This one is the cheapest.

David: It looks okay.

Ella: And it's closer to my job, but it's smaller.

David: You're right. The other one is bigger, but you will like being closer to work in the winter.

Ella: I really like this one. It's much bigger and more beautiful.

David: Of course you like it Ella. It's the most expensive. It's almost twice as much as the other one.

Ella: Maybe I could get a roommate or two. What do you think Dad? Dad?

UNIT 4　TRACK 8 and 9

David: Heather: This is a big responsibility, Nick. Are you sure you can handle it?

Nick: No sweat, mom! It'll be easy.

Heather: Okay. So remember, feed Woofy twice a day and he usually goes for a walk after dinner.

Nick: Usually after dinner. Got it.

Heather: Feed Chewy just once a day, and change his litter box occasionally.

Nick: Yuck. Okay.

Heather: Now, your brother needs to eat some vegetables at least once a day. No exceptions. And he always has to take his medicine. After every meal.

Nick: Sure. Anything else?

Heather: Water the plants every other day. Oh! And play them some music sometimes. It's good for their growth.

Nick: Music? Really?

Heather: Yes. Some smooth jazz. Never play them that stuff you listen to.

UNIT 5　TRACK 10 and 11

Ella: Hello?

Bobby: Ella where are you? I tried calling you all afternoon.

Ella: I'm sorry Bobby. I was so busy I didn't notice.

Bobby: YOU were busy. Yeah right. Where were you at 12:30?

Ella: When you called at 12:30, I was working out!

Bobby: Uh-huh. And at 1:30?

Ella: When you called, I was talking with my boss.

Bobby: Okay. And at 2:30?

Ella: Oh. I was grocery shopping when you called at 2:30.

Bobby: 3:30?

Ella: I was starving! At 3:30, I was having a little snack.

Bobby: How about 4:30?

Ella: I was studying in the library when you called. I didn't even notice.

Bobby: That's why I called! I need a ride to the library.

Ella: Oh! Well, can you meet me here?

UNIT 6　TRACK 12 and 13

Heather: What's wrong with Woofy?

David: What do you mean? Nothing's wrong with him.

Heather: But he looks so sad.

David: What? He's a dog. He can't feel sad.

Heather: Of course he can. Animals have emotions, just like people! Look at those sad eyes.

David: Heather, dear, those eyes are saying, "Feed me." That's all animals need people for. food.

Heather: David, you're so wrong!

David: When animals want something, they always give those same, sad eyes.

Heather: Well, let's not feed you and see what kind of eyes YOU make! Look at Chewy. I think he's really angry about what you're saying.

David: Now, Heather…

UNIT 7 TRACK 14 and 15

Ella: Hey, Grandpa. What're you up to?

Henry: Well hello there, Ella. I'm just working on my new hobby, Lifehacking.

Ella: Lifehacking? Okay. What's that?

Henry: Lifehacking, Ella my dear, is the art of taking common items, and finding new uses for them that make life easier.

Ella: Sounds neat. What's the sponge in the bag for?

Henry: Well, you soak the sponge in water, put it in a plastic bag, and put it in the freezer. After it's frozen you can use it for keeping things cold, and because the sponge soaks up the water, it never gets messy.

Ella: An ice pack. Wow Grandpa! I'm impressed. So, what do you use the walnuts for?

Henry: I hate it when wood furniture gets scratches on it. I discovered that you can use a walnut to fix the scratches in seconds by just rubbing it into the wood.

Ella: Whoa, Grandpa! That's so easy!

UNIT 8 TRACK 16 and 17

door creaking sound

Heather: David! David, wake up!

David: Hmrph…

Heather: David, I hear something…

a bit of a pause

David: I don't hear –

crunching sound

David: What was that?

Heather: I told you! I think it's coming from the kitchen. You see what it is…I'll listen from here.

David: No, let's both go!

loud whistling sound

David & Heather: AHHH!!!

crashing sound of pots and pans

David: Nick!

Nick: Oh, jeez, you guys scared me - was I too loud?

UNIT 9   TRACK 18 and 19

Heather: So, what movie should we see guys?

David: Well I vote for 'Cars, Guns, Girls'. It looks action packed!

Heather: It looks like there's too much violence. What do you think, Bobby?

Bobby: I don't think there's enough jokes. It just looks like explosions and car chases. I want to laugh.

Heather: How about 'Tears of a Clown'? A sad clown who finds love and laughs. It's a romantic comedy.

David: There's not enough action for me. I'll fall asleep in a minute.

Bobby: Mom. Yuck. There's too much kissing and stuff. I'll get sick.

Heather: What do you suggest, Bobby?

Bobby: Let's see 'Bear in a Boat'. A bear who rows around the world in an old boat. Looks hilarious!

Heather: Hmm. Looks a little too silly for me. But it's better than the action movie.

David: Looks interesting enough. Okay, let's do it.

UNIT 10   TRACK 20 and 21

David: Did you meet the new neighbors?

Heather: I met them all when they were moving in, and they all have nice pets.

David: So who lives where?

Heather: Well let's see. Mr. Smith, doesn't live in the middle.

David: Okay, Mr. Smith not in the middle.

Heather: There's also Mrs. Kim. She said she doesn't like cats. Oh! And there's the cat now. The cat lives in the house to the right of the dog.

David: To the right of the dog. Okay.

Heather: Mr. Smith said he's allergic to cats. And he said he wants to change the color of his house to green.

David: Okay, I'm confused. Where does Mr. Smith live?

Heather: Well, I know Mr. Smith lives next to Mrs. Kim.

David: That doesn't help me Heather. Look, who does the cat belong to?

Heather: I'm not exactly sure, but I know the cat wants to eat the fish, and she has to cross the dog's yard to do it.

David: What!?

GLOSSARY SLE 1B

A

Abduct *verb* to take someone away by force — Unit 7
Accurate *adjective* free from any error — Unit 1
Afford *verb* to have enough money — Unit 9
Amenities *noun* things around your area that make it a good place to live — Unit 3
Annoy *verb* to make someone feel a little angry — Unit 1
Apply *verb* formally request something — Unit 9
Argument *noun* a fight had with words — Unit 5
Atmosphere *noun* the way in which a place feels — Unit 9

B

Backfire *verb* an attempt that fails — Unit 9
Basket *noun* a container made of woven strips — Unit 1
Beat up *phrasal verb* to injure someone by fighting them — Unit 7
Bite *verb* to tear through the skin with teeth — Unit 9
Bitter *adjective* strong and sharp taste — Unit 8
Borrow *verb* to request something temporarily — Unit 9
Broke *verb* damaged — Unit 6
Broth *noun* clear soup — Unit 1
Budget *noun* money for a particular purpose — Unit 3

C

Cheat *verb* to lie to or mislead someone for personal gain — Unit 1
Choke *verb* to stop breathing because of a blocked throat — Unit 5
Complain *verb* to express unhappiness — Unit 9
Complain *verb* to say you are unhappy with something — Unit 4
Complimentary *adjective* free of charge — Unit 10
Compromise *verb* an agreement between two or more people — Unit 9
Content *adjective* quietly satisfied — Unit 6
Corporate climber *idiom* someone interested in becoming successful at a company — Unit 6
Crawl *verb* to move on hands and knees — Unit 6
Crunchy *adjective* makes a loud noise when broken — Unit 8
Curious *adjective* want to know something — Unit 1
Curse *verb* say bad words — Unit 6

D

Daydream *verb* to have distracting and pleasant thoughts while awake — Unit 4
Deck *noun* a floor extending away from a house — Unit 3
Depend *verb* to need someone or something — Unit 1
Depressed *adjective* very unhappy or hopeless — Unit 6
Drown *verb* to die from being covered by water — Unit 9

E

Economy *noun* the financial system of a country — Unit 3
Ecstatic *adjective* extremely happy — Unit 6
Employee *noun* paid worker — Unit 9
Escape *verb* to get free — Unit 7
Ex *noun* former girlfriend/boyfriend or spouse — Unit 6
Exceptions *noun* something not included — Unit 9

F

Factory *noun* a building where things are made — Unit 7
Family reunion *noun* a gathering of extended family — Unit 3
Flexible *adjective* able to change to a new situation — Unit 2
Flier *noun* a small piece of paper with an advertisement on it — Unit 7
Flirt *verb* to show interest in or attraction to someone — Unit 1
Food poisoning *noun* sickness from eating bad food — Unit 2
Fragrant *adjective* having a pleasant smell — Unit 8
Funeral *noun* ceremony for someone who died — Unit 6

G

Garage *noun* a building for storing a car — Unit 3
Germs *noun* viruses or bacteria — Unit 4
Get over *phrasal verb* recover from — Unit 7
Giggle *verb* to laugh quickly — Unit 1
Goose bumps *idiom* temporary bumps on the skin from cold or fear — Unit 8
Greasy *adjective* oily to the touch — Unit 1

H

Hang out *phrasal verb* to spend time together — Unit 6

I

Indifferent *adjective* without care or interest — Unit 6
Influenced *adjective* power to affect thinking — Unit 1
Instrument *noun* object that makes music — Unit 1

J

K

Knock *verb* to hit a door to gain attention — Unit 5

L

Leap *verb* big jump — Unit 1
Lend *verb* to let someone borrow something — Unit 9
Luxury *adjective* something that is desirable but not essential — Unit 7

M

Minor crime *noun* an illegal act that would not lead to jail time — Unit 3

N

Necessities *noun* something that is essential for life — Unit 7
Neighborhood *noun* the general area of a place — Unit 3
Nerdy *adjective* very interested in technical or scientific subjects — Unit 6

O

Observatory *noun* a place for observing outer space — Unit 3
Out of shape *idiom* in poor physical condition — Unit 5

P

Package tour *noun* a travel tour which includes everything — Unit 2
Panic *verb* to suddenly feel fear — Unit 1
Patient *adjective* able to endure waiting — Unit 2
People watch *idiom* observing people and their interactions in a casual way — Unit 8
Pickpocket *noun* a thief who steals from people's pockets — Unit 4
Play it safe *expression* be careful — Unit 4
Pleasure *noun* happiness and satisfaction — Unit 8
Poodle *noun* a breed of curly-haired dogs — Unit 3
Power went out *idiom* lost electricity — Unit 5
Pricey *adjective* costing a lot of money — Unit 1
Promotion *noun* advancement in position — Unit 5
Prove *verb* provide evidence for the truth — Unit 7
Proverb *noun* a well-known saying that expresses truth — Unit 1

Q

Quote *noun* the exact words spoken by someone — Unit 1

R

Resources *noun* environmental assets such as water and energy — Unit 2
Retire *verb* to end working permanently — Unit 5
Risk *noun* a chance of something going wrong — Unit 4
Rob *verb* to take something illegally from a person using force — Unit 5
Rotten *adjective* affected by decay — Unit 8

S

Secretly *adverb* not known to others — Unit 8
Sensitive *adjective* easy to feel something — Unit 8
Sightseeing *noun* visiting places of interest — Unit 2
Silver Lining *noun* something that offers hope — Unit 1
Skip *verb* to not do something you usually do — Unit 4

Social life *collocation* the time available for friends and family — Unit 5
Squeaky *adjective* makes a high noise when pressed — Unit 8
Straighten *verb* to make something into a straight line — Unit 7
Suburbs *noun* a residential district on the edge of a city — Unit 3
Suite *noun* set of rooms — Unit 10
Survive *verb* to live through difficult conditions — Unit 3
Sweet tooth *idiom* really enjoys candy and sweets — Unit 10

T

Telemarketer *noun* a person who sells things over the phone — Unit 9
Texture *noun* the feel of a surface — Unit 8
Therapy *noun* treatment of mental problems — Unit 7
Thrilled *adjective* very excited — Unit 6
Throw up *phrasal verb* to empty the contents of the stomach through the mouth — Unit 4
Ticklish *adjective* sensitive to being touched — Unit 8

U

V

Vegetarian *noun* a person who does not eat meat — Unit 10

W

X

Y

Z

NOTE

NOTE

NOTE